JUNK MALE

JOHN WEBB

JUNK MALE

JOHN WEBB

HarperCollins*Publishers*

HarperCollins*Publishers*

First published in Australia in 1998
ACN 009 913 517
A member of the HarperCollinsPublishers (Australia) Pty Limited Group
http://www.harpercollins.com.au

Copyright © John Webb 1998

Australia Council for the Arts

Written with the assistance of the Australia Council.

This book is copyright.
Apart from any fair dealing for the purposes of private study,
research, criticism or review, as provided under the Copyright Act,
no part may be reproduced by any process without written
permission. Inquiries should be addressed to the publishers.

HarperCollins*Publishers*
25 Ryde Road, Pymble, Sydney NSW 2073, Australia
31 View Road, Glenfield, Auckland 10, New Zealand
77–85 Fulham Palace Road, London W6 8JB, United Kingdom
Hazelton Lanes, 55 Avenue Road, Suite 2900, Toronto, Ontario M5R 3L2
and 1995 Markham Road, Scarborough, Ontario M1B 5M8, Canada
10 East 53rd Street, New York NY 10032, USA

National Library of Australia Cataloguing-in-publication data:

Webb, John, 1954-.
Junk male: reflections on Australian masculinity.
ISBN 07322 5883 9.
1. Men - Psychology. 2. Men's movement - Australia.
3. Masculinity (Psychology) - Australia. I. Title.
305.320994

Cover photograph: Edward Cranstone, Australia 1903–1989.
Man with spanner. c. 1943, gelatin silver photograph, 24.5 x 19.5 cm.
Collection: National Gallery of Australia; Canberra.
Reproduced by permission of the National Gallery of Australia, Canberra.

Printed by Griffin Press Pty Ltd on 79gsm Bulky Paperback

9 8 7 6 5 4 3 2 1

CONTENTS

Introduction	1
Body	23
Fathers	43
Soldiers	65
Sport	87
Other men	107
Work	127
Artist	149
Murder	171
Suicide	193
Conclusion	213
Notes	235
Bibliography	255
Acknowledgements	261

INTRODUCTION

Forward steps are made by giving up old armour because words are built into you — in the soft typewriter of the womb you do not realise the word-armour you carry.

> William Burroughs, quoted in Barry Miles,
> *William Burroughs: El Hombre Invisible*

I felt like crying, I really did. But I said to myself: 'No, not now. Not with all these people here. Pull yourself together. Not now. Not here.'

> Brian Jackson, *Fatherhood*

Everybody is interested in men these days, except men — straight men, that is. Women want to know that men have a heart and what they feel. Gay men want to know about straight men because, although they have escaped to create the heterodox, they have not escaped the dominance of heterosex. But straight men? Interested in defining and exploring themselves? Never. A man with doubts is no man at all. A man who spends his time on questions cannot be a man of action. Self-interest is self-indulgent and unheroic and has to be discouraged.

There has been a constant search in the media for the New Man, but he has remained elusive. Is the modern man 'sophisticated, sexually broad-minded, apolitical, city-bred, modern, yet still indentifiably Australian and proud of the fact'?[1] In that case he has already arrived, because this was a description of modern men in *Man* magazine in 1938. While the search continues, the quarry remains reluctant to be recognised, nervous to be named, and determined not to be defined.

The aim of this book is to explore various aspects of men's lives in order to identify and track the effects of masculinisation, particularly on men themselves, but also as an inhibiting factor in their quest for new forms of masculine identity. Biography and autobiography have been used as raw material, for they frequently focus on the rites of passage from youth to adulthood, but such material inevitably demonstrates tensions typical of men's positions, and these contradictions are discussed in the conclusion.

SELF-ANALYSIS

If a man these days is to have any social or political conscience he must ask questions, and those questions will multiply effortlessly and endlessly. There seem to be few answers and the old answers no longer work; the old assumptions about roles are no longer unassailable. They have been opened up to new and fundamental questions posed by feminism and suddenly they look like a very shoddy set of solutions, which protect masculine privilege with little justification.

Men now have to come up with new answers. If the old answers are no longer answers, or there are new questions, then men had better start finding some answers for themselves or risk losing any credibility as people involved in bringing about a change for the better. The current bewilderment of men about how to be male in a changing world can be summed up by Clive Robertson, that grumpy exponent of masculine confusion: 'The whole point is that there's no instruction book in the glovebox to tell me what to do. I don't know what to do in life. Nobody's ever told me what to do. It's just a fluke that I know about toilet training.'[2]

Productive self-analysis is not a typically masculine skill. Introspection is effete, indulgent and narcissistic. When men set out to look at their own situation, they do occasionally discover that the goals they are pursuing have little to do with what they really want. They are merely goals that they felt they 'ought' to pursue, not ones that they 'want' to achieve. It is as if men had accepted an agenda from outside and elsewhere, which defined

Introduction

what kind of person they ought to be, and that a sceptical questioning of this was not part of the plan. Other desires have been accepted as their own, and other agenda have been rejected, as they might lead to a loss of power.

Men operate within a definition of themselves as masculine that hides the mechanisms of their power. They are comfortable if they are able to discuss someone else's oppression, but once the discussion shifts to men themselves, they become anxious and uncomfortable. How is it that men might be oppressed? Surely, men are not victims? Men may be the oppressors, but they can't be victims — can they? While the mechanisms by which women are oppressed can be relatively easily seen and understood by most men, those same men struggle to detect the crippling mechanisms of masculinity in their own lives. If men are operating within a framework that obscures discussion of that very framework, then their ability to constructively analyse their own place within the patriarchy is necessarily limited.

Men have difficulty in seeing themselves and their actions because of the way their masculinity is constructed. A man doesn't see himself accurately, because his investment in the structures of masculinity means he can't, and that's the problem. Men seem to view the self as something that, once constructed, can take care of itself, as it is self-explanatory and needs no maintenance. Keith Douglas, a soldier poet of the Second World War, was challenged to state what he believed, as it appeared he believed in nothing. He replied, 'Well, I do believe in something, and I have come to the conclusion that the particulars of my creed shouldn't be examined too often. If you have something valuable, keep it in a safe place and look at it only occasionally, to see if it is all right. If you keep taking it out to play with it you'll break it or lose it sooner or later.'[3] This suggests that men see the self as a mechanism, which is created, put in place, and then expected to run for ever.

Male life is a sequence of rites of passage, each of which contains an exchange; in exchange for conforming to the mechanisms of patriarchy the male is offered some measure of power. Each little exchange confirms the male's sense of gender identity to the point where manhood is acquired. In each of the rites of passage there is a sacrifice. The male is asked to 'give himself up, empty himself to prepare to be something he wasn't by nature',[4] to give up any questioning of the self or the system, and to surrender some degree of his individuality. Most worryingly he will probably be asked to suppress some aspect of his affective side, qualities which might in general be called feminine, for in the pursuit of masculinity the male must suppress the feminine. In short, his aim must be 'the abolition of sensitivity and feelings'.[5] If Australian society has constructed an image of the feminine, then it has also constructed 'an image of maleness, of masculinity, which is frequently as limiting to the man as the image of femininity is to the woman'.[6]

MASCULINITY AND MASCULINISATION

Masculinity is a construct, a cluster of values that the developing male comes to identify with as he grows up. It is visible as sets of codes, groups of men showing certain values that can be seen by dress, physical stance and movement, vocabulary and speech. These all betray habits of mind. The experiences men undergo in order to fully achieve particular masculine styles are frequently deeply damaging to the individual male. Men have a fragile sense of identity, owing to the problematic nature of their upbringing, which leaves men with a residue of unresolved conflicts. Aware

Introduction

of the uncertainties of their status, men's underlying emotion is fear of their vulnerability, which leads to a readiness to perceive threat and to react with violence. This may be turned either inward at the self in suicide, or outward against others. Men's unacknowledged conflicts are most of the time 'left to lie underneath the surface of the smoothed out moves [of masculinity], jarring them occasionally, flaring up in surly and resentful episodes or exploding in violent anger'.[7]

To return to the idea of rites, progress towards masculinity is composed of various rites of passage, generally organised by men among themselves, and during these rites powers are conferred or promised. Central to the rites of passage is the idea of the test or trial. This may necessitate a demonstration of some skill, perhaps a physical skill, but the man or boy must show it under pressure at the site of the rite.

Banjo Paterson's poem 'The Man from Snowy River'[8] deals with a rite of passage containing a physical test, passed with flying colours by the initiate. When the absence of the horse is discovered the 'cracks', the 'tried and noted riders from the stations near and far', gather at the homestead. Not a woman is mentioned in the poem; the site of the test is strictly male, set apart from the domestic, which is dominated by women. The only three characters made individual are Harrison (the 'old man with his hair as white as snow'), Clancy, and the 'Man', but that title is not bestowed on him until after the ride.

When the riders gather for the 'fray', the 'lad' is at first rejected. Harrison, the group's leader, speaks the group's dismissal, using the galling term 'lad': 'Lad, you'd better stop away . . .' It is left to Clancy to speak up for the 'stripling'; indeed, 'only Clancy stood his friend', as he invites him to join the ride, giving him an opportunity to prove himself.

Junk Male

The horses are found and chase given, yet all the riders are halted by a steep hill, at the top of which 'even Clancy took a pull'. In the instant he decides to chase the horses down the hillside, the 'lad' becomes a 'man'. The test of courage in not even hesitating before riding down the slope, and the skill of 'racing down that hillside' and then 'wheeling' the horses to the right before they reach the shelter of the hills, are successfully undertaken, and in a quiet change which speaks volumes, the 'lad' has become a 'man' by the time he reaches the 'dim and distant hills' over which he chases the tiring bush horses. In his final apotheosis he becomes 'the Man' in the final stanza, and as is suggested by the poem's daring postscript, such paradigms of test and success have become the norm for the creation of masculinity for men in Australia ever since.

While 'The Man from Snowy River' demonstrates the rites of passage in a fictional form, here is how a 17-year-old boy from Perth, Western Australia, recalled, in a piece of autobiographical writing, his first day at a new primary school.

> I couldn't believe it. Johnny had just asked me to sit with him and his friends and within five minutes of starting I was asked to join his group, and I hadn't even tried.
>
> There was a good atmosphere around this school. I had the feeling that they were a nice bunch of kids. Johnny introduced me to his group. They all stood there and stared for a moment, I felt really bad.
>
> It seemed funny to me. The school playground was really nice with places to sit and Johnny's group sits around the back of the toilets.
>
> Johnny seemed to be the leader of the group. Two of the boys approached me and told me to sit down. After sitting

Introduction

down they turned their backs and started to whisper. When they turned around they had a lit cigarette in their hands.

They began asking me questions, to which every answer was no in my mind. They asked if I smoked. I had never smoked in my life. What was I to say? I really needed to be accepted, so I told them yes. Thank God the bell went.[9]

The male alone cannot endure being alone. He is defined only by having a place in the scheme of things, by having a place in the group. The boys withdraw to a separate place, behind the toilets. The social history of this sacred masculine site has yet to be written. Thomas Keneally, for example, can recall 'pissing contests up the creosoted walls of St Martha's boys' toilets [which] I joined in enthusiastically, straining my lower belly to get my stream of urine an inch higher than that of the bloke beside me'.[10] The only witnesses for what follows will be boys.

The isolated male 'feels bad' when he is looked at by the others in the group. He is encouraged to feel his powerlessness and inadequacy. Presiding over all this is 'Johnny', the strong presence, the leader. After initiating proceedings he recedes into the background. He is clearly the leader of the group, and he is the one whom those in the group wish to appease, or more likely impress. Pressure is brought to bear by coercive methods to make the narrator feel that black is white, as he is asked to assent to questions 'to which every answer was no in my mind'. But given his '[need] to be accepted', how can he stand alone against the group's power? It holds out the promised benefits of membership, solidarity, and action on his behalf at times of threat. He is saved by the bell, but whether he will survive the interrogation the next time is open to doubt.

Junk Male

Masculinity is singularly resistant to change from outside, but this can be explained by the mechanism of rites such as the one just described. If that boy were to become a member of that group, then he would have an interest in making sure that any subsequent initiate was inducted into the group in exactly the same way. For such rites have changed little over the decades. Here is an account by Jules Archibald of a similar experience in Warrnambool, Victoria, in 1868, more than a hundred and twenty years before the previous account: '. . . in a cave on the river to which we boys used to repair [after classes at Warrnambool Grammar] . . . I learnt to smoke Barrett's twist tobacco in a meerschaum pipe, under the auspices of the school's most senior and most distinguished alumnus, big Jack Murray, afterwards Member for Warrnambool'.[11] The details of the rite are remarkably similar: the group, the spatially separate site, the lovingly recalled means, perhaps a result of the older man's nostalgia compared to the raw need to belong of the younger narrator of the previous passage, and the presence of the 'Johnny' figure, only this time there is an explicit connection with the leader's future political power. The Johnnys of the playground are those who have found out early how to exploit the rites of passage for their own benefit, and how to create or gravitate to the centres of power.

As a social historian Manning Clark also made the connection between the social habits acquired among adolescent male peers and later life. Forced to undergo harsh and unnecessary initiation rites at Melbourne Grammar, the older Clark wrote in *The Puzzles of Childhood* of the boys of the 'Long Dorm', the group mainly responsible for creating the 'lore of the tribe' at Melbourne Grammar.

Introduction

> ... The members of the Long Dorm were the boys from whom the next batch of house prefects were chosen; they were on the first rung of the ladder of success in the school. I did not realise then the role of those young men as guardians of bourgeois society in Victoria. I saw them as bullies, as young men of whom I was scared. I had been scared before, but this, I discovered, was a super scare, like those early scares about annihilation, the scare on first confronting the men with the qualities, temperament and character of those who come to the top in every human society.[12]

It seems that the 'Johnnys' of Australian playgrounds and boarding-school dormitories are practising how to become adept at creating subtle networks of domination to stand them in good stead in adult life. The victors become the voice and acceptable face of public masculinity in Australian life, and the outcasts, the failures, are deprived of sufficient masculine status to be accorded a hearing.

THE LANGUAGE OF SILENCE

The inarticulate 'cheer' of the man from Snowy River before his dramatic ride raises the problem of expression. In the fraction of time of the test, complex exchanges are being made, usually marked by silences and suppressions rather than expressions. In unravelling the knot around speaking, men may need to examine their silences at such moments.

> Such silences are not the quiet of nature, they are a negative which are culturally and socially determined and hold the potential for meaning and living social relations. They contain

flashes of danger; dilemmas, contradictions, difficulties in the relation of the subject to others, which precede linguistic expression and therefore do not find their way into verbal expression.[13]

The danger of these silences is that they represent early difficult experiences and, for a man, to return to such sites is to risk the welling up of ambivalences which will threaten to overwhelm the fragile masculine face that that man presents to the world.

Men's silences represent an obvious place for them to start in unravelling their own masculinities. Faced by women with new vocabularies of being, they are running the risk of falling out of contention in defining themselves. They need to find a new language in order to speak of their experiences in some insightful way. If they do not, they will lose the right to speak of themselves with any authority. If they find themselves speechless when confronted by the new articulacy of women, or tongue-tied in dealing with their masculinity, then they are being defeated by masculinity's 'failure of reflexivity, the incapacity of old vocabularies to speak of new cultural and historical relationships'.[14] As it is, men are lagging desperately behind.

Men's emotional illiteracy has origins that are too deep to be reversed by a mere act of the will. 'If the vast majority of men are emotionally illiterate [it is because] ... the social construction of masculinity creates an absence, a loss, a silence at the heart of men's social relations'.[15] Such illiteracy requires more than condescension, for it is very hard work for men to speak of their feelings in any analytical way. When one man set out to interview other men about their experience of fatherhood he discovered a reticence that puzzled him. There did

Introduction

not seem to be a language of emotion available to them. When interviewed as husband and wife, the couples

> still reacted as if they were inquiring about motherhood, and it was not unusual for some of the women to answer the questions directed at the man, even to the extent of explaining what he felt. The man normally accepted this, and might act only as a spectator at his own interview ... Later when he did speak more fully, one sometimes felt the opposite dilemma; it was as if one was recording something very private.[16]

The second epigraph at the head of this introduction is a man describing his experiences at the moment of his child's birth, but it might be used to refer to any moment at which a man experiences a more than usually intense burst of emotion; the immediate response is to bury that emotion in order to maintain an unemotional masculine mask, and to become invisible behind it.

The silence into which men retreat is in no small part a willed thing. The origins of this are in our past, when convicts were encouraged to be silent in the face of punishment. Schooled in the agony of the triangle, the

> scarred back became an emblem of rank. So did silence. Convicts called a man who blubbered and screamed at the triangles a crawler, or a sandstone ... By contrast, the convict who stood up to it in silence was admired as a pebble or iron man.[17]

One convict sentenced to receive 100 lashes at one time, an uncommonly harsh penalty, managed to endure it in silence, and elicited the admiration of the overseer, who gave him a fig of tobacco, remarking 'You are a Steel Man, not a Flesh and Blood Man at all if you can stand to be sawn asunder . . .'.[18] The urgency with which Brian Jackson in the subscript to this introduction wills himself not to show emotion is some indication of the extent to which men have internalised a lack of emotion with masculinity itself. The utter sanction on tears as unmasculine can now be understood, appearing as it does so many times in Australian male autobiography; tears were for mothers and sisters, not for boys or men.

Many men have undergone the 'subjective experience of feeling thwarted by language from saying what you feel, but it is not a lack of language that is the problem . . . the self is unable to locate its relation to expressions of feeling, so they remain alien objects of investigation, rather than means of interaction'.[19] The habit of mind of hiding emotion could mean the loss of the ability to identify in language the signs of that emotion in the self. The Australian male's stoic laconism needs to be seen for what it is: a profound lack of connection with the self and others.

If men do not have effective communication with others, it is possibly because their communication with themselves is not all that effective either. If masculinity has erected a maze within, such that a man cannot know or state his desires, then that might be their first task; to open up the channels of communication with the self. If their relationship with themselves is based on subtle dishonesties, then how can they be expected to be clear in their dealings with others? 'We need to develop more fruitful relationships with ourselves in order to relate more honestly with others'.[20] For within men there is a 'wordless room'[21] which they know to be themselves, yet they have no words to act as the key to the door to the room, nor words to describe what is inside it. In writing this book I have

Introduction

become aware of 'how heterosexual men have inherited a language which can define the lives and sexualities of others, but fails us when we have to deal with our own heterosexuality and masculine identities'.[22]

To achieve some insight about masculinity is a daunting task for this reason: men must come to know themselves before they can act. This then might be the double task for men: to unlock the masculinity within themselves, then undo its effect on the people around them.

MASCULINITY AT A COST

What if men were to ask this question of their own lives: has masculinity achieved anything for us? Certainly, while masculinity has meant that power and privilege have gravitated to men, there is also a personal cost in men's lives, and if they were to ask that question in as deep and searching a manner as they were capable, then their answers might be disturbing. A more constructive starting question might be: what has masculinity done *to* men? We know from feminist analysis what it has done to women and children, but what has it done to men?

When men do look to themselves, they see themselves obeying and acting out imperatives that have little to do with what men really want, or might be able to achieve simply as people. The 'years of tight control of our emotional lives and desires have made it easier to do what we "ought" to do than what we want to do'.[23] If men were to genuinely engage in a search for what they wanted to do, the end product of such a search might be the response: what else can I desire other than that which I 'ought' to desire? What can I possibly want other than that? Such a response would merely point to the way in which men have accepted and internalised an agenda of desires not their own, rejecting any other possible agenda because that might mean a loss of power.

On their journey inward, men are likely to make the shattering discovery that the power associated with their masculine role is only promised, and never fulfilled. Masculinity is a value whose arrival is always being heralded but never quite arrives; a wished-for state always delayed. It is a perpetual future, a vision of inheritance, an emptiness waiting to be fulfilled. For masculinity can never be completely and finally fulfilled. It is always about to be proved by the next deal, the next car, the next house at the better address, and so on. It may also be taken away by other men, whereas a woman's femininity cannot be taken by another woman.

Once a man reaches this point of personal futility, all he has left is a sense of having been duped, and the bankruptcy of the masculine state. This may be a powerful factor in the male mid-life crisis. According to Dr Peter O'Connor, a psychologist who has studied this phase of men's lives, the drama of middle-aged questioning arises from the man's discovery that his 'subjectivity, his inner world, has been sacrificed to the outer world of success, power and competition'.[24] However, the man needs to question the agenda sooner for it to be truly productive in terms of life choices, and it is no coincidence that those men who are hardest hit are those who have most wholeheartedly bought the masculine dream.

The masculine ego is frequently conceptualised as a fortress, as masculinity is experienced as being perpetually under threat. Renaissance artist Leonardo da Vinci designed the perfect castle, which demonstrates the metaphor. His castle, built from

Introduction

massive masonry angled to deflect cannonballs, was protected by outlying bastions and surrounded by floodable moats. Interestingly enough, the castle's circular shape meant that all talk, even whispering, carried to the ears of the garrison's commander. It seemed that the castle was designed to withstand not only attack from outside, but treason from within. 'To maintain its identity it must not only repel external attack but also suppress treason within.'[25] To return to the opening of this chapter, to the words of the man about the birth of his own child: a man is as careful to suppress rebellious feelings from within, as he is to deflect and deny feelings from outside.

The masculine ego might also be thought of as a maze. The man himself knows it well, for he created it. However, he has forgotten the exact location of the absolute centre, so that he cannot return to it for safety, and he is only protectively lost on the periphery of the self. Thus he has at once the safety of concealment, and the chance of ambushing from that concealment, even though his own centre is concealed from him.

These two symbols, the fort that rejects and the maze that baffles, might represent the ways in which men defeat and deflect intimacy with others, especially women, for intimacy is likely to lead to the fall of the citadel of self, or to knowledge that is uncomfortable. As men are forced to reject all that women stand for, and to pursue the qualities associated with manhood, it is as if they are in flight into the protective maze or the defensive fortress, the exclusively male worlds of the club or pub, themselves defensive sites.

The most damaging encouragement of masculinisation is that to be masculine a man must stand alone. If intimacy is threatening, then to be without links to others is to be free and powerful. If a man could be above all claims on his humanity, then he would become

> the archetypal male hero, free of all ties. An independent man driven by a mission, wracked by hardship, emotionally apart, linked to the world by loyalty, duty and an abstract sense of love for a cause. He reminds us of all those other boyhood heroes who had to be free of the ties that bound them down — women, children, emotional relationships — before they could get on with doing what a man's got to do'.[26]

The sad result of pursuing independence is that at its end a man might discover that his freedom was a delusion. In asserting his own right to act free of all restraint, he was merely pointing out the limits of his own role. The men 'who live the dominant version of masculinity [become] . . . trapped in structures that fix and limit masculine identity. They do what they have to do'.[27] From a youthful belief that men would be free to do whatever they liked, they come to realise that they can do what they have to do only within the confines of their assigned masculine role in society.

The tragedy of heterosexist masculinisation is that it wounds men by encouraging the pursuit of self-sufficiency. For men need others, male and female, in order to realise their full potential, and need the challenge of a mature relationship with a woman to achieve some measure of emotional value in their lives.

What is left instead is an emotionally impoverished person with few emotional skills, inarticulate in expressing his own needs, with a pride that makes admission of need or fear equally impossible; a deep distrust of himself and his body, cut off from

Introduction

his male peers as much as his own generation of women, unable to engage in any constructive dialogue with his own self or body, let alone others', who gets by from moment to moment as he puts off again and again any radical action to stave off the collapse of the overarching personality.

The training to be masculine leads to a terrible toll late in life. The concept of what constitutes 'masculinity' needs to be relaxed and modified to allow men some measure of emotional growth so that the long-term troubles of masculinity do not manifest in men's lives in violent and self-destructive behaviour. Men need a wider permission.

Traditional masculinity is outmoded and needs to be scrapped. The concept of what is 'male' needs to be recognised for what it is: obsolescent 'junk'. It needs to be replaced by a more comfortable and timely model. As a nation we can no longer go on bearing the social cost of propping up an idea of masculinity in whose name untold psychological damage is perpetrated, as much on those who suffer in trying to live up to it, as on those who suffer from its unfettered operation in their daily lives — the women and children of Australia.

A NEW MASCULINITY

Built into feminism is a challenge to men to change and discover new forms of masculine identity, but change has its problems. When it comes to action, men are trapped in a pendulum swinging between defending men and emphatic assertions of their masculinity, and a retreat from masculinity to the 'enemy camp' of feminism. The individual man is caught in a pattern of vacillation, negotiating a tortuous and unsatisfactory course between agreeing vehemently with his women friends that all men are bastards, and being caught in a nostalgic need for the uncritically supportive affirmation of men's company. Guilt and self-recrimination, however, are not sound or enduring reasons for adopting a position, and good intentions founder on the guilt of *mea culpa* politics.

How can men find a stance that will throw out the bathwater of patriarchy without throwing out possible infant forms of new masculinity? For as long as there are boys who need to become men they will have to face the transition from boyhood to adulthood through socially established rites and forms. This represents perhaps the most promising direction: men 'need to differentiate masculinity from patriarchy and realise that patriarchy is only one undesirable and extreme version of masculinity'.[28] At present men lack a sufficiently clear view of the situation to make this finer distinction, and so everything in the broad spectrum of psychological masculinity is rejected.

Men's lack of insight about their own behaviour and how it can effectively lock others out is a major stumbling block to genuine change in relations between men and women. The obliviousness of men to the effects of their behaviour may infuriate women, but 'masculinity has a vested interest in blocking unheroic masculine self-analysis'.[29] A lack of insight by men about their own masculinity guarantees a ready supply of men to defend masculinity who have no basis for their defence beyond a vague belief that certain rights accrue to them merely because they were born male, but that lack of insight must be seen as a product of masculinity.

If men cannot separate themselves from that with which they identify, namely masculinity, they can know neither masculinity nor themselves. For men, knowing masculinity is a

Introduction

cultural task yet to be achieved. While women's understanding of their own situation has progressed and clarified with remarkable rapidity, men are far behind in their parallel task.

The words by William Burroughs at the beginning of this introduction point to what men need to lose before they can gain from change. If women have recognised that feminism's modification of society will take seventy years and will suffer reverses and diversions, then men's re-evaluating their own gender is equally long-term. For

> gender is an unfinished project . . . Too many possibilities are as yet unrealised, too many confusions have been built into our thinking from birth, to make it possible to produce some immediately complete clarification.[30]

The 'word-armour' men wear, partly inherited from the 'soft typewriter of the womb', partly due to the overwhelmingly powerful stamp of society pressing its alien shapes onto them, needs to be understood from both within and without before they can begin to see the armour as unnecessary.

BODY

What I hide by my language, my body utters. My body is a stubborn child, my language is a very civilised adult.

>Roland Barthes, *A Lover's Discourse*

'Let's swim naked,' she said.
'O.K.' But he was suddenly reminded of the film *Deliverance*. Perhaps it was the rapids and the high and thickly wooded river valley bearing down on them. He had momentary visions of them being sniped at by Northern Queensland mountain men. Not to mention dark hillbilly sexual images.
'Don't be silly,' Anna laughed. 'We're alone.' She removed her bikini, dropped it at his feet and dived into the deep pool. She surfaced and her breasts bobbed white in the shadows and reflections of the valley walls.
'Come in Stephen. Get your gear off!'
He was surprised to realise how he felt threatened by her, by her strength and independence.

>Robert Drewe, *The Savage Crows*

Sex and gender begin with the body. When we look at young children, we see bodies unmarked by the process of learning to be a man or woman; they merely are, unknowing of gender, role and sex. Theirs are guileless bodies, not guilty of borrowing the poses of others to achieve a purpose. What we envy in them is their ignorance of the cramping of personal style which comes with puberty's unavoidable choices.

Men may appear to have an uncomplicated relationship with their bodies, but the male body is a site for considerable doubts and anxieties. For boys at puberty the body becomes riven with tension; it is where they feel their masculinity as most present, but also most vulnerable and threatened, the site which must simultaneously project and yet veil their masculine style, patterned on the men whom they admire.

The body is a text which contains cues to power and domination, and these cues need to be understood and modified. Men should learn to read their own bodies; to see how the impulse to power is translated into postures that impress themselves on the spaces around them. The gaze needs to be turned back onto men.

The body is a notoriously difficult thing to analyse. Constantly fluid, rearranging itself, it defies commentary in its infinite potentiality. With this difficulty in mind I will use various sources to still the body so that it may be examined. The first of these is a very familiar masculine icon: Michelangelo's *David* (1501–1504).

THE MASCULINE ICON

The *David* celebrates the opposition of Florence to the French, who, led by Charles VIII, had earlier invaded Italy from the north. In a typical fusion of the male body and the public virtues, in this case courage, fortitude and faith, the male body is regarded as standing for the state victorious. If the statue stands for the state triumphant, how does this accord with the statue's pose?

The brief answer is that it does not. If you look at Donatello's (c. 1450) or Andrea del Verrocchio's *David* (c. 1475), the figure is shown after the confrontation. The victory is clear from the head of Goliath which lies at the feet of the successful David. In Michelangelo's *David* there is no such certainty; the action David is performing is that of taking the sling from his shoulder preparatory to the fight. This is an uncertain David, the fight yet to be fought, concentrating all his courage for the fray.

The point of view also affects the statue's impact. The block of marble from which it was carved was very shallow, and so the figure is strangely narrow when seen from the side. From in front the figure seems relaxed and balanced in the typical Greek manner; the weight on one heel, thus drawing the body into the relaxed S, so typical of the statues of antiquity. If the figure is viewed from the direction of its gaze, however, a different impression entirely is created: '[F]rom any other angle the twist of the neck seems strained, the frown uncertain'.[1] From this angle David seems to defensively recoil, turning away from threat, and revealing significant doubts. Though the Greek models from which Michelangelo took the pose were of perfect gods, this statue is 'human, mortal and contradictory . . . This ambiguity gives the figure great inwardness, an inner tension expressed across the whole of the body'.[2] One critic has drawn attention to the way in which the statue embodies the 'medieval concept of the open and vulnerable side, opposed by the closely defended active side, while the head is turned to look in the direction from which attack may come'.[3] What seems at first to be a statue that endorses an uncomplicated masculinity turns out instead to be one that looks forward to the contradictions of modern masculinity.

THE MANLY STANCE

Boys at puberty will model themselves on an admired older male, perhaps even copying poses, ways of moving or standing, from one whose masculinity they wish to borrow. In doing so they connect with a tradition of projected power, and further extend it into their own generation. So imitation can be one means used to create a masculine presence during the precarious rite of crossing from boyhood to manhood. Another means is the creation of an entirely new stance. In learning to use his new body, the boy–man will experiment with pose and stance in order to arrive at his particular new and unique way of projecting male power.

An example of the former method of creating a manly stance is James Dean. As an actor coming from the Midwest to New York he was particularly aware of the need to fashion a new self to be noticed in the competitive world of acting. His observant actor's nature meant that he was aware of the flexibility of his body, and he knew that with practice he could achieve a new version of himself, using his body as a 'conscious vehicle for the expression of that fabrication of the self, the personality'.[4] One form of experimentation was photo sessions with Roy Schatt, best known for the famous photograph of Dean in Times Square. Schatt records that at one session Dean said '"Wait a minute, I want to try something." He turned his head slightly to the left and looked down. I asked him what the hell he was doing, it was such a strange pose. He said, "Don't you see it? I'm Michelangelo's David."'[5]

By the time we see James Dean as Jim Stark in *Rebel Without a Cause* in 1955, leaning against the black Mercedes in his red jacket, he is no longer the innocent, vulnerable farm boy. His pose is 'not just a pose. It's a warning, a sign'[6] of his carefully constructed but now hidden masculinity. This may explain the impact of James Dean on the younger male generation of that time; he visibly expressed their projected yearning for a stable masculinity. The irony of his stance was that it was derived from such an ambiguous model as Michelangelo's *David*.

An example of the latter method of self-construction is Winston Churchill. His biographer described him, when a young man about to enter Sandhurst, as 'small in stature, with thin, unmuscular limbs, and the white delicate hands of a woman', a build which was, by Sandhurst standards, 'quite inadequate'[7] and when a contemporary met Churchill in 1903 he described him as a 'little square-headed fellow of no very striking appearance'.[8] Yet by 1940 this unprepossessing boy–man had transformed himself into a symbol of resolute defiance fitting Britain's need to see such a leader. This pose was achieved by sheer practice and determination, a 'deliberate decision and iron will'. As he told his doctor, 'I can look very fierce when I like'[9] and there is every possibility that he actually practised his

Body

famous oratorical postures in front of a mirror before using them in public.

ADOLESCENCE

Puberty is a period in life when changes in the body force the owner to come to terms with it, even if their particular response is to ignore or deny certain events and various changes that occur. For the boy child, puberty can be an anxious time. The body appears to rebel and mutiny, flouting the conscious control of the owner, and sudden bursts of growth cause morbid self-consciousness. As the power of the body grows, its owner must learn how to use it anew, as an increase in bodily power means the possibility of new skills previously impossible. But it is a difficult period, as for every new skill or strength bestowed, a weakness or sensitivity may be created which may cancel out the former. For boys, puberty is not a simple liberation into new regions of power and status; it can also be a frightening door into enduring uncertainty and anguish.

Going swimming can be the trigger for deep fears about the physical self, especially about the time of puberty. The source of such anxieties is usually comparison with another male. The visible achieved masculinity of one body will be the source of despair and depression for the undeveloped body's owner. David Meredith, the hero of George Johnston's semi-autobiographical *My Brother Jack*, admires his brother's body. As the growing David records the changes in each of their bodies, he relentlessly catalogues the way in which, even though he may be taller, he is not at ease in his body and turns away from it, unlike Jack, who is a sportsman, a boxer, and later sexually confident. Here is how the mature narrator describes his changing body:

Junk Male

> In the twelve months after I left school a dreadful, phenomenal thing happened, and my grotesque skinniness, with the pimples that came about this time, made everything immeasurably worse. I stopped going swimming that summer because I was convinced that everybody was pointing out my skeletonic shape, that every giggle or guffaw was directed at me. I began secretly to buy physical culture magazines, but cancelled the order after I had taken three issues because the comparisons were so shattering. I saw myself as the perpetual figure captions 'Before', never as the muscular Hercules captioned 'After.'[10]

The significance of always being 'Before' and never 'After' is that it seems that David Meredith is eternally trapped in an immature vision of himself. He can never achieve the careless self-confidence of the mature 'Hercules' of the body-building advertisements.

If fat is a feminist issue, then muscle is a masculine issue. Men are encouraged to pursue hardness in the body as much as women are allowed to be soft. But hardness of body also connotes the ability to hold things out. Muscle becomes the means to repel or expel things ranging from accusations of effeminacy to feelings themselves. The musculature operates as more than just the outwardly visible symbol of male power; it is also symbolic of inward rigidity and invulnerability.

Sam Fussell, in his account of suffering and recovery from the 'iron disease' of body building, *Muscle: Confessions of an Unlikely Body-Builder*, describes how he set out to create a 'human fortress' for himself in his own body in order to protect himself through adolescence, for a 'muscle vocation was the answer to my private panic'.

Body

> The threat wasn't just from without; it was also from within
> ... Who was this man who cried not just at graduations and
> weddings but during beer and creditcard commercials? Who
> was this man terrified of his own rage, his own greed, his own
> bitterness? Who was this man who never heard a compliment
> without hearing a subtextual insult, who never said 'I love
> you' without resenting that other fact; 'I need you'. I couldn't
> deny it was me, or could I? There wasn't enough pomade,
> mouthwash, deodorant and talc in this world to eradicate my
> sins, but what if I created a shell to suppress them?[11]

So he sets out to grow muscles, and the 'more I grew, the more I felt protected, insulated from everything and everyone around me', to the point where 'the muscles kept everyone at bay. Not just the muggers and street thugs, but friends and family, even dates'. What he and the other gym junkies did was to create their own world of regimentation and control, for 'as long as we created for ourselves a rite of passage, we could instil our lives with meaning'. In doing so, however, he becomes a 'prisoner of body-building, a victim, an iron casualty of the sorriest kind'.[12]

Saddest of all, his physical development has not allowed for any equivalent spiritual growth.

> I felt that if you could somehow find a chink in my armor and
> pry apart a muscular pauldron from a gorget, you'd find
> nothing within that vast white empty space but a tiny soul
> about the size of an acorn.[13]

Repelled by this vision of his own spiritual poverty, Fussell quit the body-building scene and wrote his book as part of his recovery.

Hardness is bound up with another part of the male body, the penis. In the early stages of puberty, when anything can trigger an erection, even while he is asleep, the adolescent boy suffers a distinct disorientation of attitude towards his body and behaviour. Behaviour is supposed to do with control, choice and intent, but here is a part of his body over which the boy has no control, which moves and stirs on a whim, and which has intentions of its own. As discipline is forced on the mind, the body insists on its own frequently contrary and capricious logic.

MIND, BODY AND PENIS

Few men will recall or admit the imperative effect of an erect penis in that period of time between discovering its function in erection and its use. The Australian writer Eric Rolls has described it in this way:

> My most lasting memory of adolescence and young manhood is of an erect penis . . . It poked holes in my underpants. I would sit in a tram. Vibrations from the wheels travelled through the seat, through my buttocks into my groin. Any movement excited it. I would feel the head nudging against an unmended hole. I would try not to think about it. That aggravated it. The head prodded harder, broke through the hole and snared itself like a Bearded Dragon lizard in wire-netting. I would will it to subside so it could extricate itself. Concern for it caused more engorgement. The corona flared over the hole. Good God! It would cut off the return of blood and go gangrenous, a genuine fear. It seemed prepared to hold its head up throbbing for hours. The clear, miraculously slippery cleansing fluid would begin to ooze out of it. It came

Body

in beads. I could feel every millimetre of the progress. Before it choked its head off, it would have time to soak a great shameful patch in the front of my trousers. I would watch from the tram for a hotel with a side entrance to its lavatory — I was too young to go through the bar — then leap off at the next stop, subdue the penis and release it.[14]

What is of interest here is that the penis is described almost as another entity which communicates with the boy through suggestion. At the time there seems only to be an 'on' switch: 'The penis itself projected erotic visions on a screen behind my eyes. It had automatic control as well as conscious control that worked the on switch only.' It is only subsequently that the boy learns of the association between his erections and the possibility of sex with the opposite sex. This period of apparent random arousal and response, however, can be extremely disorienting and shaming for the boy.

The lack of any conscious control over erection leads to the adolescent boy regarding his penis as something outside the normal frames of reference of behaviour, but at that moment a split has occurred between body and mind, for the boy begins to identify the penis as something outside himself, something 'separate, down there, apart, not a part', and as 'having a life of its own, leading the man on almost in spite of himself'.[15] The difficulty of the rest of a boy–man's life is to discover a union between the mind, body and penis so that they are able to live together in relaxed harmony. This is unlikely when the growing boy is surrounded by a culture which encourages and promotes the phallic view of the body, and priapic modes of behaviour. Priapus was the Roman God associated with erection, and was represented with a gigantic erection, or sometimes just as an erect phallus. In modern terms the priapic myth is the 'performance principle', which means that a man 'must be ready for sex no matter what the immediate circumstances or feelings'.[16] To be always erect is as tiring as having a permanently hard musculature; such display is ultimately exhausting.

Part of men's alienation from their bodies has its origins in the way in which boys learn to deal with erection. The penis is at once a source of a pleasant sense of well-being, and the source of potential weakness. All too often the former is pursued in a tight, shut, blinkered way, and the latter denied. While the world abounds with images of the phallus (the gun, the knife, the fist, the skyscraper, the car) there are few images that celebrate the variety of the penis when quiescent. Recognition of the pathos, vulnerability and ludicrous nature of the relaxed penis would lead to a radically different view of its function in the life of its owner. The male genitals are 'fragile, squashy, delicate things; even erect the penis is spongy, seldom straight, and rounded at the tip, while the testicles are imperfect spheres, always vulnerable, never still'.[17]

For a man to be relaxed and passive is a source of massive anxiety, for what then might enter their bodies? It means identification with the feminine, and that he is to be worked upon, rather than working, for intercourse can be regarded at its most degraded as 'alienated work, the instrument of that work being the male body, or more precisely the erection'.[18]

It is too simple, however, to assume that the ability to achieve or maintain erection is the end of anxiety for men in validating sexual identity, as a brief examination of the process of localising response as expressed by erection will show. Interviews with pre-pubescent boys indicate that erection

Body

occurs under 'various conditions of risk, peril, hazard and threat'. Among these are 'accident, anger, being scared, being in danger, big fires, fast bicycle riding, fast sled riding, hearing a gunshot, playing or watching exciting games, boxing and wrestling, fear of punishment, being called on to recite in class and so on . . .'[19]

At this stage little girls don't even rate a mention. It follows that the connection of erection with an appropriate heterosexual focus, the opposite sex, is learned through a pattern of elimination and conscious emulation of models. Erection, which originally occurred in situations of threat and danger, is transferred and focused on the opposite sex, and some of the anxiety of the original stimuli carries over to that new focus.

The adolescent erection, however, is such that the involuntary erections achieved can be so distracting and disconcerting that they trigger even more panic and anxiety, which in turn can make detumescence quite impossible, to the point where 'his gender anxiety and his reflex erections become linked'. Thus the boy learns to 'desire such erections because he experiences them as a resolution of his gender anxiety, at least temporarily'.[20] So whether quiescent or erect, the penis is the site for a range of conflicting and contradictory signals to a man about his gender identity, and even erection does not lessen the complexity of the relationship between mind, body and penis.

THE CAPTIVE BODY

The photographs of Australian Rules players on the sports pages of the daily newspapers show ways of projecting the self that can be related to the way in which men present themselves at other times. The photos are cropped so that the frame is full of bodies, usually at climactic moments of challenge and confrontation such as taking a mark. The focus on such encounters reflects the nature of the present-day game, but what is remarkable about the photos is the intense concentration of the players on the ball, which is usually within the frame, balanced on or just out of reach of a player's fingertips.

Part of the pathos of such images is how the men in them are seen as lonely and isolated within the action. The focus is rigidly outside themselves in their watching the ball, and this separates them from one another. One of the functions of the game is to reject public display of co-operation between men. Here is how one commentator sees the playing of games between men:

> Every line of every muscle from the jaw and neck, forearm and buttock down to the calf is drawn as tightly as a bowstring. Consequently the whole body is held together like a clenched fist. It is the moment of maximum effort privileged by almost every image of sport in popular culture, a privilege that is now coming to be granted to women, so long as they conform to the masculine ideal. We [men] like to think of our bodies as being natural, but these . . . men, far from being outside culture, are deeply organised within it. They may seem animal but their bodies are carefully controlled . . . In this image the masculine body is seen as existing for itself and against others.[21]

If we make the connection between the space within the four edges of the photo and the four walls of a room, then a man on entry into a room will aim for the same impact: immediate

Body

domination of that space by the intense projection of his presence into that space. It is the kind of projection that makes women in the same space feel uneasy and intimidated.

I have mentioned ugly or troubling male bodies, and in this context it might be of interest to look at 'Victoria's most unwanted man'[22] as an example of a man who made use of his body to highlight his problems of self-presentation in the world. Garry David, who was sometimes known as Webb (no relation to the author), was unique in that he was the only person who had had an Act of Parliament framed specifically to keep him in prison. He was kept in various high-security institutions in order to prevent his escape, as he had threatened vengeance in different forms on various people and groups. He carried out more than '80 acts of self-mutilation to demonstrate his bitter hatred of authority. He slashed his arms and legs, drove nails into his feet, cut off his penis, plunged bones through his left eye, removed and consumed both nipples, and severed his achilles tendons at least five times',[23] as well as swallowing a 23 centimetre television aerial.

Within the rigid masculinity that prevails in prison, David was protected by his fellow inmates, who respected his hatred of authority. His mutilations were almost a compilation of biblical wound sites; the feet, eyes, and arms as well as the penis. Condemned to be powerless and have no authority over his body, he sought to reverse the situation by taking his body hostage and making a martyr of himself. What he did was to dramatise the male body as a site of profound psychic pain. His imperfect, gaunt and scarred body was a more honest testament to the anguish of uncertain masculinity than the solid-muscled presences adorning the sports pages of the daily newspapers.

The wounding of a body is an opportunity for its owner to achieve an enhanced and enlightened view of the physical self and this is certainly an element in people's reactions to injury and illness. Similarly the potential of a wound for psychic growth can reveal the poor and mis-aligned relationship a person has had with their body as they respond fearfully to the dormant psychic pain.

A wounding is a chance to be reborn in a new form. If recent films are any indication, though, if men are wounded or nearly destroyed physically, they are simply reborn in an even more powerful form than before. The hero in *Robocop*, for example, comes back with his body converted into impenetrable armour. What we see is a masculinity so bankrupt of ideas that it can be remade only in the old mould, though more powerful. Wounding is not to be explored as an insight into vulnerability or mortality, it is to be exploited to create a more concentrated essence of masculinity. This might explain the appeal of Ned Kelly to generations of Australian men. The pain of being wounded is to be denied in the conversion of the body into a machine so that the problems associated with the presentation of self through a damaged and pain-racked body can be forgotten.

PAIN AS CATALYST

Illness has the effect of making the sufferer more than usually aware of their body, but then men do not do particularly well when forced to become aware of their bodies. In Robert Drewe's collection of stories *The Bodysurfers*, the pun of the title on 'body's surface' is explored in one of the central stories of the collection, 'Stingray'.[24] While bodysurfing at Bondi, David, the main character, is stung by what he believes to be a stingray. He struggles ashore and manages to drive back to his apartment.

Body

The hand 'throbs with a power all its own [till it] dominates the room; it seems to fill the whole flat. He wishes to relinquish responsibility for it as he has done for much of his past life'. Concerned that he may be poisoned, David considers who to ring; Angela, his ex-wife, who would be 'cool in a crisis', or another friend, Victoria, who 'has mentioned recently at lunch that her present relationship is in its terminal stage'. He chooses Victoria, and 'in ten minutes she is running up his stairs, panicking at the door with tousled hair and no make-up, and ushering him into her Volkswagen'. In the casualty ward of the hospital they witness a girl who has overdosed being stomach-pumped back into consciousness and reluctant life. David, however, remains sullenly within himself, as the symbolic parallel of the suicide's saving eludes him.

He and Victoria, whom he puts into the caring role which she fulfils so well, begin a relationship, and the painful episode is put into the past. Nothing has been learned from the wound. The symbolic awakening of the would-be suicide passes David by, and he merely rearranges the former elements of his life. The wounding, which was a chance to become more aware of himself, is lost as an opportunity to develop a more profound awareness of himself and his state of being. David falls back into adolescent patterns and, rather than taking some kind of control over events and his body, allows a woman to take that role. He does not achieve the break with his past life for which the pain might have acted as a catalyst.

For the observant man, however, a literal wounding is a chance to restructure his attitude towards the self. The damaging of the external envelope is the opportunity to submit the internal self to a re-examination, and the results can be most positive. One recent work which tells of such a process is Tony

Junk Male

Moore's *Cry of the Damaged Man*. The book is subtitled 'A Personal Journey of Recovery' (from a motor accident), but it is not merely an account of the physical process of recovery. It is the account of a man using the shock of an accident to completely re-assess himself and his life. It is a case of change and damage to a man's body forcing him to reconsider how he interacts with the world, and how much of that interaction is based on bodily practice.

The accident, followed by the enforced isolation of the intensive care unit, cuts Moore off from the comforting routines of his life as a doctor, and forces him to indulge in extended introspection. Infantilised into helpless immobility by his extensive injuries, powerless over his own body and situation, he begins a re-assessment of his life.

It begins with his self, and the need to dominate the events around him. A brief memory loss has the effect of reducing the 'relentless dogmatism which had previously affected my conversation'. He goes on from there to look at his role and place in the family. First of all, as father he sees that his children need him to be 'strong and available', which he has not been, and so he sets out in his convalescence trying to 'improve [his] fragmented fatherhood'. As a husband he comes to recognise the faith and patience shown by his wife, who has had to put up with the 'compost of emotional confusion' which his life has been. Though at first he resists it, he can later admit that he has 'become passive, truce-seeking and conciliatory'.[25]

Central to Moore's account is the awareness that an accident can 'smash open a body and break open a life',[26] and that the resultant matter of healing is not just a matter of fixing the body. What the event has alerted him to is that the wounds he has to deal with are not all visible.

Body

Accidents, especially motor vehicle accidents, are often seen as turning points in the narratives of men's lives, but more for the process of recovery, during which they have the leisure to engage in extended self-examination, than for the accident itself. In accounts of such accidents, though, the focus is on the dramatic moment of collision rather than the much longer, less overtly heroic period of convalescence and rehabilitation. Jeff Kennett and Bob Hawke are just two prominent Australian men who have been involved in severe road accidents which they claim changed their lives and attitude to life. Here is how Bob Hawke's biographer described the motorcycle accident in Kings Park, Perth, which nearly killed the young rider:

> He remembers the bike going into a skid, being thrown from it and landing hooked through with agony. He lay on the side of the road, screaming with pain. After some time a passing motorist took him to hospital. Apart from bruising, Hawke had no sign of injury but was in unbearable pain; 'I was screaming and screaming it was so unspeakable. I thought, death would be marvellous. I'd have deliverance from this.' Injections eased his agony down to a black labyrinth. Inside it he was left, entombed.[27]

But it is possible that from that 'black labyrinth' enlightenment may come.

The masculine body, then, is the site for a good deal of anxiety, which we attempt to conceal with postures of power pushed out into the spaces about us, so that neither we nor others will turn the gaze on us to detect the fragile and vulnerable self behind the display. The body is the envelope in which we reside and which we must inhabit in our dealings with the world. Much as we may, for a host of reasons, distrust or misuse our bodies, in the end we must negotiate through and with our bodies. The challenge is to find ways of achieving insight into our physical selves so that we can see ourselves from the outside and put our bodies in a new perspective.

FATHERS

What is a father, a real father? What is the meaning of that great word? What is the immensely great idea behind that name?

Dostoyevsky, *The Brothers Karamazov*

Though people said I resembled Father, I couldn't connect what I saw with the red-faced man who walked in from harvesting with a straw hat and hanky knotted round his neck, let alone the man I saw in the wedding photos which moved around the bedroom according to Mother's moods.

Chester Eagle, *Mapping the Paddocks*

INDIVIDUALISATION

In Western society, becoming an individual is seen as the process of becoming independent from the major influences on one's character, namely the mother and father. For the boy who would be a man the mother must be denied and the father's power challenged and rejected. The following summary describes the process:

> All infants begin life in a primitive symbiotic relationship with the mother or surrogate mother. The eventual task of development is to differentiate oneself from one's mother and to become a separate individual. Commensurate with its physical growth, the infant develops psychological capacities which enable it to differentiate between similarities and contrasts, and to discriminate between 'inside' and 'outside'. Eventually the child becomes aware of the difference between outside objects, including its mother and others, and itself, thus enabling it to be aware of self and non self. At the same time the child is learning to differentiate between others and itself, it is also modelling itself on the mother, i.e. identifying with the mother. The various fundamental tasks such as walking, talking and holding objects are learned, in fact, through imitation of the primary caring person, the mother. Of course, the imitation is modified by the child's mental and physical endowment. Thus identification with the mother is the beginning of identity and the basis from which later identifications are formed. What is

important to our understanding of male gender identity is that in order for a boy to develop masculinity, he must first give up his identification with his mother and identify with his father. This task is further complicated and made difficult because the boy may not wish to give up the 'security given closeness' that identification with the mother provides.[1]

It follows from this that there will be fewer problems for a girl associated with the leap forward into maturity. They have the benefit of a same-sex role model in the mother as well as a parent who is also present and emotionally available in real terms. A boy on the other hand must first disengage from the mother and then re-engage with the father as the focus of his understanding. This will mean that he will simultaneously feel that he has been betrayed or abandoned by his mother or that his love for her has been rejected, and that his needs, now projected on the emotionally or actually absent father, are now not being met in as direct or real a fashion. The destabilising effect of this switch of allegiances means that the boy is likely to experience a good deal of ambivalence towards his mother, himself and his father about his newly problematical gender.

The ramifications of this change in alignment for the boy are far more profound and longlasting in the boy's life than the equivalent changes in a girl's. If in forming his sexuality the boy must break away from the mother and pattern himself on his father, he loses twice: in rejecting the mother he loses the deep affective links with his emotional yardstick, while in seeking to emulate the father he condemns himself to perpetual conflict and frustration. In turning away from the mother towards the father, the son substitutes competition for co-operation, and discovers distrust where formerly there was deep bonding.

Fathers

Once the primary identification with the mother has been sundered, the prospect of oneness with another may come to be perceived as a regresssive step. Therefore much male behaviour, with its emphasis on autonomy and independence, may be seen as the hysterical rejection of need or dependence. For to be male is to be separate. 'The ways and means by which each man resolves these issues of separation and identity will determine his capacity to risk himself in intimate relationships and to allow the expression of feelings and desires which hitherto have been feared and denied.'[2] For too many men, needing another, especially a woman, is seen as tantamount to annihilation. This may explain why a man may infuriate a woman by appearing to move towards and then away from her in a pattern balancing 'merging' and 'separation'.[3] A man may repeat this alternating pattern, as 'in his effort, albeit unconscious, to deal with the first wound, a man will return over and over to a scene which closely simulates that original scene'[4] of apparent rejection. It may not be a coincidence that the infancy-to-separation period and the length of many love affairs is about eighteen months to three years.

THE 'ELSEWHERE' FATHER

There may be a huge gap between a man's belief about his role and place and the reality of the family's operation. Fathers may believe that they are meaningfully involved with the family's day-to-day dramas, but wives and mothers may have a very different perception of the total experience.

> Even though men will often say that their families are the most important thing for them since this is what they are

Junk Male

working so hard for, women will experience it quite differently. It is difficult for men to break with an instrumentality [that of work] that has come to dominate so much of life. It is as if men are often not available in relationships, their thoughts constantly drifting off. Real life and real work exist elsewhere, so that it can be hard for men to put their energies into relationships. Often we arrive home too exhausted, drained and used up. Our best energies have been used up at work and we rarely hold ourselves back so that we have something to give when we get back.[5]

So to the boy the masculinity represented by the father is 'both mysterious and attractive in its promise of a world of work and power, and yet, at the same time threatening in its strangeness and emotional distance'.[6]

When a father is actually present there is no guarantee that he will be emotionally available. American writer Paul Auster describes talking in adulthood to his father as

a trying experience. Either he would be absent, as he usually was, or he would assault you with a brittle jocularity, which was merely another form of absence. It was like trying to make yourself understood by a senile old man. You talked, and there would be no response, or a response that was inappropriate, showing that he hadn't been following the drift of your words. In recent years, whenever I spoke to him on the phone I would find myself saying more than I normally do, becoming aggressively talkative, chatting away in a futile attempt to hold his attention, to provoke a response. Afterwards, I would invariably feel foolish for having tried so hard.[7]

Fathers

There seems no real way of communication taking place somewhere between the mystery of silence and the assaults of 'brittle jocularity'.

Whether one parent is absent in actuality or just emotionally unavailable, the consequences for a child's development are serious, for if 'one of the parents is absent for some reason there is a gap in both the internal reality and the psychological development of the person'.[8] Looked at from the child's perspective, the absence of the father creates problems of perception and understanding. As the father is 'divorced from the day to day care [required in family life] it can mean that fathers become unreal and idealised figures who only enter the family as authorities or else to ensure separation'.[9] As the boy observes it, the father is absent from the domestic sphere, engaged in an activity which seems somehow central and crucial, the world of 'work'. On his return the father punishes ('You wait till your father gets home!'), engages in nervously physical horseplay, or is an exhausted figurehead at the dinner table. So to the boy the masculine world is at once mysterious and attractive, promising work and power, and yet also threatening, in that it means absence and distance. The example of the father 'attracts and repels in dynamic contradiction'.[10] The boy must negotiate the tensions of this opposition of the son's need for a firm male presence in his life and the father's distance and emotional indifference.

One power that the father's absence hands to the mother is that she is free to interpret the father to the son, as she 'stands between him and his father, and colours his vision of the masculine world'.[11] In so many families it is the mother who is the principal representative of the family culture by which the family is sustained. Manning Clark, for example, found his mother was 'full of instructions on how to behave',[12] but this power to interpret reveals itself in far more subtle ways. What frequently occurs is that the son sees a father who has a public position of power (as did Manning Clark's father, who was a Methodist minister), yet who possesses little or no power in the domestic sphere. In his courtship of Manning Clark's mother, Clark's father soon found himself 'like a prisoner in the dock answering charges',[13] and to the young Manning they resembled 'she the judge, and he the accused', or were like 'gaoler with a prisoner, a prisoner who is sometimes given an exeat to go fishing, play cricket, or watch a football game'.[14] This is one of the most complex 'puzzles' of Manning Clark's childhood; to reconcile his father's private and public personae, and achieve some healing vision of his father's life.

GOD OR MORTAL?

The break between son and mother, and new awareness of the father, is experienced by the son as a battle, as much a battle he must fight for himself and his allegiances as a battle carried on over his head for definition of him. Manning Clark's life was a battle between his father's view of him as 'the thoughtful customer', and his mother's view of him as 'a very special boy' marked by special weaknesses. Eventually Clark perceives that it is a 'neverending clash of wills, she striving to confine me within the walls of her world, and I catching glimpses of another exciting world'.[15]

At first boys need their fathers as omnipotent gods in whose powers they can rejoice. As Manning Clark said, 'my father was my first enthusiasm', though he is honest enough to go on with hindsight to say further that he 'could not live without an enthusiasm, painful though it has always been to

Fathers

discover the reality behind the myth my brain conceived to feed the hungers of my heart. There had to be an idol'.[16] The approval of a god is more powerful than that of a mere mortal. If we set our fathers up as absolute in their power, then the moment at which a son detects a fall can be a significant event in a child's developing view of the world as a complex place where ambivalence is the norm rather than the exception.

Popular culture reflects the ambivalence that surrounds fathers, and many modern films revolve around the search by a male character for a stable and benevolent father figure. In *Star Wars* Luke Skywalker's quest ends with his confrontation with Darth Vader, the 'dark father', and in *Terminator 2* the 'terminator' of the title becomes a father of sorts to the lost boy figure. One earlier film, that states the difficulties of father-and-son relationships, and looks forward in a very prescient way to the present day in its depiction of the depowered and yet decent and sincere father, is *Rebel Without a Cause* (1955). The film is a rite of passage of a boy's journey into maturity; Nick Ray, the film's director, summed up the film's mood and plot in one brief production note: 'A boy wants to become a man, quick.'[17] The character sketch for Jim Stark, the youth whom Dean plays in the film, could equally be a summary of the troubled adolescent male today:

> Jim. The angry victim and the result. At seventeen, he is filled with confusion about his role in life. Because of his 'nowhere' father, he does not know how to be a man.[18]

One of the film's discarded scenes deals with the ambivalent feelings towards the father figure in a boy's life, and the combination of need and hostility that the figure occasions.

Junk Male

> I wrote a scene where Jim was talking to his parents [said Stewart Stern, the film's script writer], and suddenly you see a shooting gallery in an amusement park ... and there on the moving belt instead of ducks were his mother, father and grandmother, in 3D. They were balloons, but very recognisable. He took aim and missed Mom and Grandma, but he got Dad right through the head and all the air went out of him, out of the balloon. Suddenly, Jim was in a panic about what he had done, and he leapt over the rail and grabbed the balloon, threw it in his car, raced it to a service station and said, 'You've got to fix this, you've got to fix it!' And they've got the tire inflator out and they start patching this thing up and pumping it up, and they get it half pumped, but the air just keeps on going out of it.[19]

This scene reveals the contrasting emotions of the son: the urge to reduce the inflated image, but simultaneously the need for the maintenance of that image while the other problems that face the son are overcome.

There are two scenes which are crucial to an understanding of Jim Stark's father, and Jim's relationship with him. In the first scene, the first occasion on which we see the father, he is dressed in his suit from work, but he wears an apron and is cleaning up some soup that he has spilled on its way to his wife. Jim's imperative need for his father's direction emerges in this scene, when he asks his father for guidance:

JIM: Can you answer me now?
FATHER: Listen, nobody should make a snap decision — this isn't something you just — we ought to consider the pros and cons.
JIM: We don't have much time.

Fathers

> FATHER: We'll make time. Where's some paper? We'll make a list.
>
> JIM: (*shouting*) What can you do when you have to be a man?
>
> FATHER: What?[20]

In the last scene featuring Jim's father he tries to work through with Jim the consequences of the accident caused by the 'chicken run', a test — one of many for Jim Stark — he has just been involved in.

> FATHER: You know you did wrong. That's the main thing, isn't it?
>
> JIM: No! It's nothing! Just nothing!
>
> FATHER: Son all this is happening so fast.
>
> JIM: You better give me something, Dad. You better give me something fast . . . Dad? Aren't you going to stand up for me?[21]

As sons we are all waiting for our fathers to 'give us something', but frequently the gift is withheld, and when our fathers die we only then discover our own ignorance.

Many sons may spend their lives waiting for a sign of love from their fathers, but perhaps others wait also for the knowledge, the hidden knowledge of masculinisation, to be passed on. Such a statement as 'I'll explain that to you, boy, when you get older',[22] frequently reiterated, may have a devastating effect in the long term, in that it creates unrealistic expectations, as it did for Manning Clark. While a father may make a conscious and consistent effort to pass on practical skills which he believes will help his son to 'be a man', he may at the same time fail spectacularly to give him sufficient guidance about how to feel as a man. Manning Clark comments on his father that he

> gave us [Clark had an older brother] much advice on how to play a straight bat ('There are only two strokes to learn in cricket, boy; how to play forward, and how to play back'), on how to make a late-cut or a leg-glance, how to tie a fish hook, how to split wood ('Aim for the grain, boy, and then it's as easy as cutting butter with a knife'). He never told me how to behave. Perhaps life had so filled him with doubt that he no longer believed that he had any lessons to impart.[23]

This is the particular fear that our father's resolute silence on the important matters creates: the realisation that perhaps, as John Mortimer the English writer said of his father, 'he had no message'.[24]

THE FATHER IN AUTOBIOGRAPHY

Australian fathers seem to get a fairly bad press from their sons in autobiography. In *The Watcher on the Cast-Iron Balcony*, Hal Porter has seen only two corpses in his life, one through a 'lens of tears', the other through eyes 'dry and polished as glass'. The former is the body of his mother, the latter that of his father.[25] George Johnston's biographer Garry Kinnane is moved to open his biography with a detailed refutation of the impression created by Johnston's semi-autobiographical *My Brother Jack*, in which the father is presented as a cruel and sadistic man who regularly beats his sons with a razor strop and threatens his wife with a revolver. He says rather that Johnston's father was really a decent and respected man, who disagreed no more frequently, and certainly no more violently, with his son than most fathers would.

Kinnane is more revealing when he looks for a motive for such a portrait, suggesting that 'there are indications that this was done for revenge', and that the writing involved 'distortions of childhood memories, some deliberate and some probably unintentional, representations of strong feelings, and a considerable degree of pure invention'.[26] What we may be looking at in autobiographies by men, therefore, is the need to give a rendition of this difficult relationship from the son's side, rather than one concerned with absolute truth or compassion.

In this light Xavier Herbert's account in his autobiographical *Disturbing Element* (1963) goes more directly to the heart of the matter regarding the difficulty of a son presenting an image of his father. After having chronicled his father's abrupt temper and his use of physical punishment, he can go on to say

> he was really a mild man. Yet I literally made a monster out of him. I mean I made him into one in my imagination. Even long after I'd come so far from fearing him as to pity him, the monstrous symbol that stood for him in my sub-conscious being still lurked there, watching, menacing, a great bull-thing.[27]

This account's more naked treatment of the buried and unresolved conflicts of the father–son relationship goes far to explain why Johnston's portrait might have elements that shocked the surviving members of his family. But then again, Johnston would never have gone as far as Herbert, who bluntly states 'my father was my enemy'.[28] Herbert's account is the more convincing in its suggestion of the continuing fight that every son, within himself, has with the shadow of his father. We are so often trying to overthrow or simply evade the power of our fathers; it is just that the writer gives a public account of that process.

One area in which one might expect that fathers would enjoy some communion with their sons is in a shared enthusiasm for sport, and to an extent this seems true. Manning Clark recalls that, when the crystal set had been tuned, which required a sensitive touch and no-one in the room to move,

> my mother and sister were not allowed in the room during that sacred hour when an announcer was reading the results of the football, or the scores in the cricket. 'God spare me days, woman' . . . my father would say to my mother if she dared to interrupt our male communion. We three males assumed my sister had no rights or interest in the 'man's world'.[29]

In a more profound and far-reaching way, spectating could be an affirmation that all was in its place, and that all was well with the world. Chester Eagle's father took him to see Bradman bat in the first Test series after the Second World War. As Bradman walked to the wicket,

> to my surprise, Father, along with thousands of others, stood to clap. I had never dreamed that my shrewd, disbelieving Father was capable of hero worship, and I realised that someone he passionately believed in was making his way to the centre. Bradman walked more slowly as he approached the pitch. He took block, straightened, tugged his cap, acknowledged the applause, then bent over his bat.[30]

Fathers

This experience is of the hierarchical nature of the activity. The son is surprised to see the father, whom he reveres as a hero, as having a hero. Thus, when Bradman is once more back 'where he belonged', the hierarchy of rightness extends from Bradman, through the father, to the son, and the son clearly and positively experiences his place in the order of things.

THE TERROR OF AFFECTION

To a child the usual forms of fatherly approach, a kind of good-humoured, physically robust play, can seem intimidatingly aggressive. Though the intention may be to demonstrate affection, the effect is often to terrorise. Such a moment is the return of the father in George Johnston's *My Brother Jack*, as seen from the young David Meredith's point of view:

> The climax of it all came when a strong voice, hoarse with excitement, began to shout, 'Minnie! Minnie!', and without warning I was seized suddenly and engulfed in one of the gigantic, coarse clad figures and embraced in a stifling smell of damp serge and tobacco and beer and held high in the air before the sweating apparition that was a large, ruddy face grinning at me below a back-tilted slouch hat and thin fair hair receding above a broad freckled brow, and then there was a roar of laughter, and I was put down, sobbing with fear, and the thick boots marched on and on, as if they were trampling all over me.[31]

The 'stifling' of the child by the 'sweating apparition' indicates how the post-war generation was overwhelmed by the spectre of war brought home by their fathers, but in the gesture of holding the child aloft like a trophy there is the terror experienced by the child. While the moment of reunion may have been remembered by the father as a joyful one, for the child it is an occasion for a fear of annihilation, as the 'boots marched on and on, as if . . . trampling all over me'.

In dealing with affection or moments of high emotion, fathers are less effective. As Manning Clark is left at Melbourne Grammar as a boy at the start of term, he prays, desperately, that he might not cry that he is being deserted by his parents, though he still does, earning the contempt of his brother, but 'father, as ever, pasted over anything embarrassing or painful by saying we would all laugh about it one day'.[32]

For all his skill as a preacher in the pulpit, his father can be reduced to impotent silence by Manning's mother's tears:

> My mother begins to cry . . . Tears stream down her cheeks. She says to me, 'Mann, dear, perhaps God is punishing me for what I have done. Perhaps I should not have let you go to Melbourne Grammar.' I do not know what to say. I am in the presence of something I do not understand. My brother tells my mother, 'Don't cry, Mum dear. I can't stand it when you cry.' My father is silent.[33]

ARRESTED PATTERNS OF CONFLICT

Too many men fail to go beyond the facile rebellion witnessed by the modern idea of what a father–son relationship is. This means that the relationship is arrested at a very immature stage, and in very negative and unproductive modes of behaviour. This establishment of patterns of conflict which remain unbroken long afterwards informs a reading of Donald Horne's *The Education of Young Donald*. One thing that 'young Donald acquired from his

Fathers

father was a passionate faith in frank and open discussion, so that later in life he could not meet his father without becoming involved in an angry argument'.[34] Here we see a situation where early habits in a relationship so dominate that the protagonists are subsequently unable to break out of them. The tone and form of the relationship had arrested in the form of conflict.

The challenge for a man is to go back and make his relationship with his father into something better, based on true mutual respect and genuine exchange, rather than the unproductive models of conflict that seem to dominate our perceptions of such relationships. It is a challenge to both fathers and sons, because it may involve actual apology and recognition of wrongdoings and abuse by both sides, but beyond that initial move lies a much more rewarding and mature friendship. As with older brothers, fathers can help enormously in our lives. To reject their knowledge of the life that lies before us is to reject a vast body of knowledge that lies readily available for our use. From planning for superannuation to parenting, from child care to car care, our fathers are people with whom we can talk easily.

The difficulty, though, lies in actually coming to terms with our fathers and what they symbolise to us. We cannot avoid confrontation at some stage in our lives, but I think it is far better to do our repair work while our fathers are alive, than when they are dead. Elia Kazan, who directed James Dean in *East of Eden*, put it clearly when he said

> one hates one's father, one rebels against him; finally one cares for him, one recovers oneself, one understands him, one forgives him and one says to oneself, 'Yes, he is like that' . . . one is no longer afraid of him, one has accepted him'.[35]

Junk Male

But it would seem that there are comparatively few men who 'recover' themselves sufficiently to go beyond their early immature pattern of behaviour with their fathers.

GENERATIONS OF MEN

The difficulty for a man, caught between the desire to identify with and yet break away from the masculinity of the father, is at once to acknowledge the influence of the father, and yet go beyond that influence. For 'in all social classes becoming a man involved striving to go beyond, and intuitively accepting the imagined world of one's father'.[36] The 'imagined world' needs to be accepted in order to be absorbed, then the son–man can begin to 'go beyond' to a new self, taking on board what is best about the father and rejecting all that is unhelpful.

If the relationship fails through opposition, then the links that might be forged between generations are constantly being broken, and nothing is learned. Each generation of men is condemned to reject the knowledge accumulated by their fathers and live out again the same errors and failures.

The pathos of so many sons and their response is that they do not discover the need that they had for their fathers till after the father's death. David Malouf's novel *Johnno* opens with the son's being forced to confront the memory of his dead father, as he dutifully arranges his father's business affairs. His first discovery is that his father had painted some raw silk bed covers with red and yellow poppies of a 'gaudy opulence which seemed all the more extraordinary because my father had painted them at twenty when he was a member of Brisbane's toughest rugby push'.[37] This prompts the son to consider that he had 'forced upon my father the character that fitted most

Fathers

easily with my image of myself; to have to admit to any complexity in him would have compromised my own. I chose the facts about him that I needed'. Therefore the son comfortably selects the father's skill at athletics, his passion for building things and his lack of literacy as comforting contrasts, but in rejecting his father's example in such typically masculine areas of activity the son has created a 'gap between us and left my notion of my own independence utterly uncompromised. Now suddenly I was not so sure'. His father's talent for walking on his hands, 'strutting about like some exotic bird, carrying his body through the air as if it were plumage, heavy, extraordinary', may, in its inversion, be symbolic of the life that the son has come to lead, and the life that he will explore through his relationship with Johnno.[38]

William Orton, father of the famous gay playwright John, better known as Joe, ended his life

> shut away in an old people's home, [where] life was even more remote than in the park greenhouse ... Existence was reduced to small memories and idle chat with old men and women who sat like corpses in the red straight-backed chairs of the Smoking Room ... He had never impressed himself on life ('I never seemed to get anywhere. I was always a failure'), and now he was fading slowly out of life with tepid, brutal anonymity ...[39]

The only personal possession that William kept was a

> photograph of 'his John' on the formica bureau of his antiseptic room overlooking the car park. The picture was of John aged eighteen, taken just after he went to RADA; a suave

smile contradicted by the boyish olive-smooth complexion and the shock of straight black hair curling like a comma across his unlined forehead.

When John was murdered by his homosexual lover, William heard about it not from a family member or close friend but from television.

> It was typical of William's life and luck. He had loved his son but never connected with him. Even the plants he cared for never seemed to flourish. 'I didn't think I was a good gardener. It upset me. I didn't tell anybody. Always kept it to myself.' William wanted only one thing in life; a greenhouse. He never got it.[40]

Keeping the photo of 'his John' by him is a sign of how the relationship had been arrested at the point of John's departure from home. The subsequent events in John's life — his becoming Joe Orton, the famous playwright, his coming out as a homosexual — are all denied by the photo.

Fathering presents us with at once our greatest challenge and potentially our greatest contribution. It is a significant challenge to go back and remake our relationship with our own fathers in a more positive form, thus rejecting the negative images culture presents to us of the father–son bond locked in conflict. How this is done is up to the individual male, for he will know his father at least as well as, if not better than, himself. To find our way to manhood (including fatherhood) is to go through the example set us by our own fathers and examine and assess its effectiveness in our lives. To reject our fathers is not to learn; it is to condemn ourselves to repeat their mistakes for lack

Fathers

of insight. To contribute as fathers we must take up the role, get involved, overcome the distance, be ourselves and provide new and stable models of masculinity for our children, whether they be sons or daughters. This is the greatest contribution we can make to the refashioning of masculinity in our lifetimes.

In his epilogue to his autobiographical *Puzzles of Childhood*, Manning Clark, in reviewing his life, ends with a dream of his father, in which Manning is standing on

> the shores of the Styx waiting to be ferried across to the other shore. My father rowed over from that shore, and started to collect bait for fishing. I asked him to help me cross over to the other shore. He replied: 'Boy, that is one journey you must make yourself.'[41]

In a moving tribute to the powerful impact of this dream and how his father's death was a milestone from which he subsequently measured his progress, Clark then goes on to say that his 'teaching in Melbourne, Canberra and Harvard, the books on the history of Australia, the book on Henry Lawson, and the short stories, are all interim reports on that journey'. In Franz Kafka's 'Letter to His Father', written while his father was still alive but not published in the lifetime of either, Kafka steadily lists his father's shortcomings as a person and father, but then concludes by saying

> my writing was all about you; all I did there, after all, was to bemoan what I could not bemoan on your breast. It was an intentionally long-drawn-out leave-taking from you, only although it was brought about by force on your part, it did take its course in the direction determined by me.[42]

Junk Male

Though as sons we may journey alone, we still measure how far we have come, and from where we began, by reference to our fathers.

SOLDIERS

I was a 'new boy' in the platoon, a reo ... I wanted to be accepted by the other guys. I wanted to do well and not stuff anything up.

Stuart Rintoul, *Ashes of Vietnam*

God be with you Love for all Time ... Remember me to baby when she is Born — if a boy don't make him a tin soldier but should war break out, let him enlist & do his bit if not he'll be no son of mine.

Captain A. McLeod (killed in action 5 December 1916) in a letter to his wife

War as rite of passage

In their readiness to answer their country's command to become soldiers, men demonstrate their addiction to the supreme test of masculinity represented by war. This testing was strongly desired as a collective test of the nation's manhood, as well as the individual soldier's. Whole generations of Australian men have had their masculinity confirmed and their importance in the national culture established by war. The example of former generations of Australian men is immediately available within the family, and knowledge of the war's causes or the issues at stake is almost irrelevant. Here is one man's summary of his knowledge of Australia's involvement in Vietnam:

> I had no idea where Vietnam was and no idea of the causes of the conflict but thought that if Australian troops were to go there then it must be right, and I would like to go myself.[1]

This Australian, Terry Burstall, in analysing his reasons for thinking thus, makes the connection back through his family:

> Most of the men in my immediate family were returned soldiers and my stepbrother and I were captivated by their magical stories of wartime exploits.[2]

For Burstall 'the notion that a young man had to go to war to prove himself [was] popularly accepted in those days'.[3] To take his place as a man in his family setting he needed to go to war and it would be a dominant rite of passage for him, as for generations of other Australians.

It cannot be forgotten that Australia, which has always seen itself as a male nation, achieved a kind of collective national manhood by its involvement in the First World War. War was seen as a rite of passage for the nation from untried immaturity to tested manhood. A writer in the *Argus* on December 1915 expressed it thus: 'It was at Gallipoli that our young and untried troops . . . quitted themselves as men, and gained the plaudits of the world.'[4] Thus the First World War, and Gallipoli especially, was the rite and site by which Australia gained its national masculinity.

From that time, the example of Australian soldiers in the First World War has been felt by every successive generation of our nation's soldiers. (Writing of the Vietnam War in *The Battle of Long Tan*, Lex McAuley subtitled his book 'The Legend of Anzac Upheld'.) This example has been at once a boon and a curse. It has meant that many men have felt that it is the 'right thing to do' to enlist, and it has set a narrow definition of what constitutes 'The Anzac Tradition'. Part of this is sheer physical presence. Compton Mackenzie wrote of the Anzacs in the First World War when he saw them on Gallipoli:

> [S]uch litheness and powerful grace as the Anzacs possessed did not suggest the parade ground; their beauty, for it really was heroic, should have been celebrated in hexameters, not headlines. There was not one of those glorious young men who might not himself have been Ajax or Diomedes, Achilles or Hector. Their almost complete nudity, their tallness and majestic simplicity of line, their rose-brown flesh

Soldiers

burnt by the sun and purged of all grossness by the ordeal through which they were passing, all these united to create something as near to absolute beauty as I shall ever hope to see in this world.[5]

In the public mind physical magnificence is part of the archetypal Anzac, along with other qualities such as courage and deadly effectiveness in battle.

SHAPING MYTHS OF MASCULINISATION

Whether in memoir, autobiography or fiction, accounts of war tend to be shaped: authors take their material and then fashion it to create a narrative. Most narratives of war follow a similar pattern, and what has been written about Vietnam is no exception. In the conscious shaping of war narratives we see the unconscious structuring of the experience to fit the masculine dimensions of the site (the foreign battlefield) and the rite (first battle, the endurance of fear, wounding and death), which means that what we read are myths of masculinisation. The experience of war follows the sequence of the typical male rite of passage, but on such a scale that it can be seen as the ultimate masculinising activity, involving the entire nation.

The Vietnam War narrative does not quite follow the First World War models such as Frederic Manning's *Her Privates We*, because Vietnam was a war that defied convention. The concept of 'battle', for example, was no longer applicable. A battle, according to the tradition of its representation in military history, was a specific site, from which the name was taken, over which there was an engagement lasting a day or part thereof, at the end of which there was a clear winner.

Instead of 'battle', Vietnam spawned the term 'contact' to cover brief but intense firefights which might last less than a minute. In the absence of battles the memories of veterans tend to cohere about isolated but recurrent events such as the first action and being 'under fire', or the wounding or death of a mate. In recollection the soldiers will often use as their central thread a particular memorable patrol.

Creating soldiers begins with their training. The process is designed to mould a group of men from different backgrounds into one cohesive group. Probably the smallest self-sufficient group in the modern army is the battalion, which has always been the basis of recruitment for the Australian army.

> It can feed itself, care for its sick and wounded. It has medicos, cooks, grocers, storemen, postmen, policemen, engineers and clerks, who record all things great and small. And to fill the needs of the human spirit a battalion has a padre and a band — bugles and colours to give mystique, beauty and dignity to its ceremony.

This is how Henry Gullett saw the 2/6th Battalion in the Second World War, and the Australian involvement in Vietnam was still organised around battalions which were rotated for tours. If training has been entirely successful, then it may be said that the battalion 'implies a state of mind . . . perhaps even a state of grace', and to say '"the Battalion thinks" or "the Battalion feels" . . . is not an exaggeration'.[6] The battalion becomes the 'Battalion family' as David Hay, the historian of the 2/6th Battalion, calls it, with its 'family stories'. The battalion is a utopian vision of masculine self-sufficiency.

Soldiers

The aim of training is to submerge the individual in a corporate identity, with which the individual can identify and become totally loyal. This group identity will be most visible on battalion parades:

> A Battalion Parade is really just a highly orchestrated yelling exercise. Almost everybody with rank around the place gets to yell at some point. The platoon sergeants yell at their platoons to get them right dressed and looking sharp, then the platoon commanders take over and yell a little more, then the platoons of all four companies are marched onto the parade ground by their respective CSMs [Company Sergeant Majors], who then hand the companies over to the Company Commanders. Some form of yelling accompanies all of this. Then, when everybody is lined up correctly and inspected for dirty boots and long hair, the RSM [Regimental Sergeant Major] yells at everybody from the front platform and hands the whole show over to the CO [Commanding Officer] ... It can be quite a spectacle, though to what purpose it is difficult to explain.[7]

The lesson to be learned by a soldier involved in all this would be the hierarchical nature of the organisation, as smaller units are handed over to larger units and higher authority.

The savagely authoritarian Warrant Officer is the staple of war narrative, and in this respect the fiction and memoirs of the Vietnam War are no different. But through all the experiences comes a disturbing ambivalence towards these archetypal authority figures. The power that they represent is at once coveted and hated.

In the fictionalised memoir *Nasho*, by Michael Frazer, the platoon meets

Junk Male

> Sergeant Porter [whose] uniform is always perfect, his greens starched and ironed till they shined. He was tall and thin, yet what there was of him was all muscle. Always straight up and down with a ramrod straight back, even when he marched . . . But above all he has the aloof countenance of one who is meant to be in charge. Everyone likes him . . .[8]

SOLDIER AS ROLE MODEL

Sergeant Porter is the figure in fiction, but such men also act as powerful role models for their direct family in reality. One Vietnam veteran was influenced to join by the example of his grandfather:

> He was a very fine, very clean cut sort of man who always had the right answer. No matter what you asked him, he was always worldly and wise. Very Army, regimented, a major who had the most fantastic handwriting. It was magnificent.[9]

In a world of confusion and uncertainty as to the role and position of men, he has the right and exact answer. No wonder he was such a powerful role model.

In John Carroll's novel *Token Soldiers*, there is also a Warrant Officer, aptly named Neil Savage. He is first met by the reader as he readies for a fight, and he is known by

> every soldier who had trained at Singleton . . . Possibly the most hated man in the Army. He was perfectly brutal and completely without feeling. He made men run until they fell, and when they could not get up again he would kick them until they did. While he was not a particularly big man, he had his weight in all the right places and if you were foolish

> enough to fall over where he could see you, you would to your cost see evidence of that ... He was very steady and calm and confident deep within himself.[10]

This appearance of being 'confident deep within himself' comes from his settled sense of being indisputably masculine.

The portrayal might lead a reader to think that such a character would be disliked and feared, yet on patrol he performs superbly and keeps the platoon together, so that the narrator must grudgingly admit, in a tribute to Savage's masculinity, 'he may be the biggest bastard alive, but he's got balls, all right'.[11] On that same patrol, when the platoon is in camp, Savage tells stories.

> He was evidently a first-rate story-teller, seasoning his yarns with a good mixture of fact and impossible fiction. Some of his punch lines brought great howls of derision, and for an hour or more he held court in this way. He would finish a tale, wait a few minutes in silence, smoking, and then inevitably someone would say, 'Come on, Sarge — tell us another one'. That was all he was waiting for, and away he would go again.[12]

Looking at the faces of the men surrounding Savage, the narrator sees 'expressions of — well, idolatry, is about as close as I can place it'.[13] The figure of Savage superbly encapsulates the mixed feelings of unformed men when faced by an icon of intense masculinity.

Army life is full of rituals. These may be overt and formal, such as the battalion parade so far mentioned, or they may be covert and informal, immediate responses to circumstances improvised by the men themselves, such as the habit of 'dousing' of new rank badges in the mess after they have been awarded. Generally such rituals are to do with induction and celebration. Some informal rituals, on the other hand, are to do with harassment and expulsion, covered by a particular Australian term, 'bastardisation'. It was generally the man who stood against the process of militarisation who was attacked and ostracised in ways specifically designed to humiliate him and denigrate him sexually:

> I can remember our OC asked the entire squadron about two weeks prior to embarkation did anybody not want to go and there was only one person and he was a regular soldier. It was on religious grounds as far as I can remember and to our everlasting shame I suppose that ninety-five per cent of us called him a coward, gave him a hell of a time.
>
> He was a nervous wreck after that. They did some rotten things to him — the boot polish on the privates, scrubbed him in the showers, incredible name calling, that sort of stuff. Really gave him a hard time. It was bad news. He cracked. He ended up with the Army psychs and a discharge so he did get what he wanted, but at what cost to him.[14]

The coward is the man who is so unnerved by the imminent test that he will do anything to avoid it. Looking back on the event, however, the man recounting the above story can add the comment, 'now probably we'd all pat him on the back for his guts'.[15]

MATESHIP

It would be impossible to talk of war and Australian men without mentioning mateship. It is a cliche of the war narrative

Soldiers

that in training, men from disparate backgrounds are welded together into a fighting force. 'It's hard to believe that in six or seven weeks a group of civilians, country and city boys, could knit together as a group and become soldiers and so close in that short time.'[16] Relationships formed under the pressures of preparation for war have dimensions of homoeroticism never fully articulated in the accounts of those who took part. The military way of life has always 'segregated millions of young men at the height of their potency, forcing them to adopt a life of close companionship devoid of female companionship', thus giving rise to what has been called 'emergency homosexuality'.[17]

The existence of such close relationships did have one profound effect. Many conscripts lacked a clear reason to fight until they saw a mate wounded or killed. One veteran who lost a mate said

> I had no scruples from there on in, no compunction whatsoever to do whatever I had to do, no second thoughts about it. They didn't have to worry about me doing my job because I had a good reason then to do it, apart from the fact I was a soldier and it was expected of me. I had a good personal reason then to do it and to do the best I could do it and as effectively.[18]

The death of a mate, therefore, became a touchstone of the reality of the conflict.

Letting revenge become a motive for aggression solves a problem that soldiers have to face, which is overcoming the reluctance to kill. After the Second World War the American general S. L. A. Marshall wrote *Men Against Fire*, an examination

Junk Male

of the stresses soldiers face in battle. Marshall concluded that there was a difficulty in making a man ready to kill, when he

> comes from a civilisation in which aggression, connected with the taking of a human life, is prohibited and unacceptable. The teaching and ideals of that civilisation are against killing, against taking advantage. The fear of aggression has been expressed to him so strongly and absorbed by him so deeply and pervadingly — practically with his mother's milk — that it is part of the normal man's emotional makeup. This is his greatest handicap when he enters combat. It stays his trigger finger even though he is hardly conscious that it is a restraint upon him.[19]

The phrase 'practically with his mother's milk' implies that compassion is a feminine attribute, as is the fear of aggression which his mother has 'expressed to him so strongly'. One Vietnam veteran recalls a Company Sergeant Major saying of a unit '"Everything's going well, but you've got to get a little more aggro in you". I thought, that's a funny thing to say; why is he saying that?'[20] The summoning up and direction of aggression is at the centre of the masculine nature of war.

Talk of aggression is all very well, but what holds men together when they must fend for themselves on the battlefield? According to General Marshall it is the fairly simple operation of a basic male response. Given masculine company and a test to be undergone,

> men are commonly loath that their fear will be expressed in specific acts which their comrades will recognise as cowardice ... When a soldier is known to the men who are around him,

Soldiers

> he . . . has reason to fear losing the one thing he is likely to value more highly than life; his reputation as a man among men.[21]

In other words, a unit in battle coheres because each member of it is concerned to keep up his own self-esteem as a male, and all are vitally involved in propping up their collective masculinity.

LOSS OF MANHOOD

If the battlefield is the place for the unrestrained exercise of learned masculine aggression, it is also the site for anxieties of emasculation. The wound to the groin is the one to be feared most, as it strikes at the soldier's sexuality. Here is a response from a soldier who believed he was wounded in that place:

> I can still remember lying there and feeling the blood running down my knee onto my thigh. I immediately thought 'Oh no', and stuck my hand down my trousers and felt the old fellow; it was full of blood. I was more worried about my balls than I was about my legs or whether I was going to die or not, because if they got me in the balls I wanted to be dead.[22]

This is the wound called

> the wound of wounds, the Wound [for] whenever a shell landed in a group, everyone forgot about the next rounds and skipped back to rip their pants away, to check, laughing hysterically with relief even though their legs might be shattered, their kneecaps torn away, kept upright by their relief and shock, gratitude and adrenalin.[23]

One promise implicit in the soldier taking up arms is that a grateful nation would show its respect in honour, public ceremony and enduring monuments. The Australians who went to Vietnam expected to take their place in the Anzac pantheon. One Vietnam veteran went to an Anzac parade with his medals. He

> came face to face with an old guy in Victoria, at Mordialloc RSL, and this guy had I think about five rows of six medals on each row and he said, 'Put those things in your pocket, son.' This guy had everything, he was unreal. 'We earned it,' he said, 'You didn't. Wait until you've earned some.' He was an old Rat of Tobruk so I guess he was entitled to say that.[24]

Despite having 'done the right thing' the Vietnam veterans were not met with respect, and their illusions were thoroughly shattered.

GENERATIONS' FAILURE TO CONNECT

There is a lesson that has to be learned by each generation of men: war is not a glorious pursuit that will bring manhood and honour from one's society. To return to the fathers and grandfathers and their function as role models, this lesson has to be learned anew because there is no effective link between the generations: each generation of men that has gone to war is held up as a silent example to the next. Bob Gibson recalls:

> My grandfather was shot through the lung in the First World War. He died when he was twenty. His picture was on the wall at home. I idolised him. He looks identical to my father and I've got the same set of eyes and everything as him.[25]

Soldiers

This veteran did not need to be told what was expected of him; the lesson had been so completely internalised that it was stamped on the face.

There is no effective communication between the generations of men about the experience of war. This is where the taciturnity of men, one of the prime qualities of the Australian male myth, works against the complexities of men's involvement in war being passed on to the next generation. One Vietnam veteran met his grandfather again.

> I looked at my grandfather and he sort of looked at me and then looked away. He had served in the First World War, in the Light Horse. He was wounded, and he's never told me much about it, but from what I can gather he saw quite a bit of action. I think I looked at him as if to say, 'Well, what should I do? You ought to know.' But then he wouldn't know any better than I do. He just looked at me and then sort of let it go.[26]

Evidently the role of war experience in sustaining masculine self-identity was as problematic for the First World War soldier.

This failure to connect between generations of men is a great loss. It represents at once an opportunity for mourning the loss or damage to the self on the part of the father, and a chance to share in understanding on the part of the son. If the connection is not made, then a chasm of incomprehension has opened. Gerard Windsor's story 'My Father's Version of the Nurse's Story' shows what can happen when such communication occurs.[27] The story is semi-autobiographical, as the events described can be independently verified. The father has been sent in search of a group of nurses, who have been held as prisoners of war by the Japanese, to bring them back by plane. The plane lands and taxis through the long grass to where the nurses are waiting under an awning. The co-pilot pushes open the door for the narrator's father to step out. The significance of the door is made clear from the father's response to the son's question of why he went first:

> I wasn't just going through any old sort of door. Damn it all, if it's dangerous or difficult or a man can be of some use, he goes first. Doesn't he?

This is the masculine code for which the son admires the father. This is the moment at which the father and the story break down. The father 'stands back, and tries to stand further back, but he cannot'. And he gives way to tears as he is 'forced to watch and hear everything'.

> And willy-nilly, I am tied to him and caught also. It's no good, no good at all. My father and I sit there and cry away together.

This crying together symbolises many things: the father's joining in the 'horror and joy' of the reuniting of Matron Sage and her nurses, his pity and helplessness at the event on the one hand, and on the other the affirmation of a link between father and son. Despite their differences of age and profession, the two can overcome the pride inherent in such roles, and effect some genuine sympathy across the illusory divide. The exchange of vulnerability is mutually uplifting.

Bernard Szapiel, a Vietnam veteran, keenly felt his inability to be loving towards his son:

Soldiers

> I've shown him very little affection. I've found it difficult to relate to him and to my wife. When he's asleep I go into his room and just smother him with affection and kisses, something that I've found very difficult to do. I think to myself, 'You poor kid, why should you be tormented like this?'[28]

The love that the veteran seeks to show his son sounds like the kind of love he himself desperately needs, to effect a healing similar to that which occurs between the narrator and father in Gerard Windsor's story. The grief that each experiences is for the lost skill of connection.

FULFILLING THE MASCULINE MYTH

Soldiers are poorly equipped for their return to society. Vietnam veterans were returned with dazing rapidity to suburban Australia, which highlighted their changed personality to those who had known them best before their departure.

> When I came back the first reaction my parents had was that here was a man that has no feeling, cold totally cold. When I'd left I was a really affectionate, home-loving person. I love my parents, I love my sisters — I used to remember their birthdays, special days, gifts, kisses and cuddles — but when they came to pick me up at the airport I just stood there. I didn't know what to do. I had no tears. I had no feeling. It was 'I'm here', and that was it.[29]

But perhaps all the problems of their return originated in the dangerous promise contained in the rhetoric that surrounded their going; that their nation would honour them as fully achieved men in the warrior tradition. This was not so, and thus the promise was revealed to be worthless. From this has sprung a sense of grievance based on the impression that the nation was insufficiently grateful.

The individual man's recognition of his own masculinity is a fragmentary and haphazard process, but for soldiers the moment of discovery can be instantaneous. Talking of a day when his platoon had a very serious firefight, an Australian veteran of Vietnam said

> that was the day I think when all the blokes who were there could say they really became men. I really do believe that. There's not too many people could point to a day and say that's when they became a man, but by Christ, I never felt so old and so drained of everything.[30]

For men the spectre of war, either survived and confirming masculinity, or unendured and thus leaving a cavern of self-doubt, is the skeleton in all our cupboards. The house in which the hero lives as a child in George Johnston's semi-autobiographical novel *My Brother Jack* must stand for all Australian homes:

> There was no corner of the house from the time I was seven until I was twelve or thirteen that was not littered with the inanimate props of that vast and shadowy experience, no room that was not inhabited by the jetsam that the Marne and the Somme and the salient at the Ypres and the Gallipoli beaches had thrown up.[31]

The novel is dominated by the narrator's shame at his failed masculinity faced by the Second World War, as he receives

Soldiers

adulation for his status as a war correspondent rather than for actually fighting.

We are now witnessing a shift in attitude to the wars we have endured as a nation. The veterans of the First World War have dwindled away and those of the Second World War are ageing, while the Vietnam War is undergoing a resurgence of interest as it is refashioned into an acceptable part of the national warrior myth, despite the evidence for Vietnam having been a socially divisive period of our history, equalled perhaps only by the conscription debates of the First World War. There is now a statue outside the Australian War Memorial, the Vietnam War Memorial on Memorial Drive in Canberra has been unveiled, and it appears the Vietnam veteran will receive the same respect and place accorded to the veterans of previous conflicts in which Australia has been involved. At the time it seemed that Vietnam was the war that would end the importance of war for Australia as a means of asserting our national identity, but, if as Peter Pierce claims in *Vietnam Days*, a 'nation's willingness to participate in war is predicated upon its population's perception of the national experience of previous conflicts',[32] then it seems that the national memory for war is short.

The elevation of the Vietnam veteran has been the result of a steady shift of opinion, for there was a time when the Vietnam veteran was positively ostracised. But if 'heroes are a social creation [and] are made by a configuration of circumstances and needs that lie outside the heroic moment',[33] and if a myth modifies current events by 'colouring men's ideas of how they ought "typically" to behave',[34] then once again we can see how men's actions are influenced by previous generations of men. In interpreting the actions of men, the aspects of their character which best fit the masculine myth are selected and highlighted in order to maintain it. Perhaps we should remember the words of Jock Simpson's sister Annie on reading Irving Benson's biography, which created Simpson's legend in the popular imagination: 'NEVER for a moment could I have visualised you would write such a FAIRY STORY.'[35] Men need to be especially sceptical when faced by exhortations to join uncritically in endorsing the values of their forefathers.

This was recently given dramatic form when Sir Edward 'Weary' Dunlop's funeral in Melbourne coincided with the auction of the Victoria Cross of Kevin 'Dasher' Wheatley, one of the four awarded to Australians in the Vietnam War. 'Dasher' won his medal posthumously for absolute bravery in the face of the enemy.

> He had fought single-handedly against the enemy and at the same time dragged a wounded man across a bulletswept field to comparative safety. Then, in spite of the opportunities to save his own life by escaping into the undergrowth, he chose to remain in the face of almost certain death.[36]

In the face of such actions it is difficult to comment; we cannot comprehend why a man would risk death to stay with a comrade. Yet what counts in these circumstances is not the actions, but how the masculine culture employs them.

'Weary' Dunlop and 'Dasher' Wheatley are appealing because their actions can be directly linked with the myths of the First World War stretcher-bearers who combined masculine qualities of bravery under fire with the feminine attributes of compassion and care for the wounded. The stretcher-bearer stood for the values of the culture for which he was fighting, by his

Soldiers

valour and compassion, his humanity and the rough exterior that disguised it . . . The rightness of the cause depended on a balance between the ferocity of the Australian soldier and the compassion . . . The Anzac soldier had to be soldier who could love as well as fight, who carried in his heart — however well disguised — the civilised values that made the Empire worth fighting for . . . Hardness and softness, fierceness and tenderness, were routinely coupled in the description of the Anzac. The coupling was an important part of the epic formula.[37]

In celebrating 'Weary' Dunlop and 'Dasher' Wheatley, then, we are celebrating the direct inheritance of the Anzac myth by the Second World War and Vietnam generations of soldiers.

Appeal to past effective modes of masculinity is a pressure to which Australian men are particularly prone. This is a sign of the bankruptcy of masculinity in modern Australia; we are eternally looking back to times of stability and cohesion rather than facing the chaotic present and the fluid future. Masculinity, militarism and conservatism go hand in hand. We must avoid the siren voice of soldiering as a solution to our uncertainties.

SPORT

People really notice when a bloke doesn't go at it flat out. It's the first thing they spot and it makes you look bad. When it's crunch time and you're backing into the pack waiting for the express train to come . . . well, you don't want to be seen not to do it.

Terry Wallace, former Hawthorn footballer

When you stop playing it's a bit like stepping over the edge of a cliff. There's nothing there any more.

Kelvin Templeton, former Footscray and Melbourne footballer

THE TEAM

Through their involvement with that basic sporting unit, the team, young men will learn a lot about sharing masculine behaviour and the tensions and trade-offs between the individual and the group. The single player must efface and subordinate himself to the team; he must show 'love of the jumper', and sacrifice time spent with others for the sake of the surrogate 'family' of the club. Even though teams are composed of individuals of roughly comparable ability, any individual brilliance is dealt with by being subsumed within the team's goals. The cyclical nature of sports that follow the seasons reflects the way in which men's sports are presented: stable, eternal, necessary, as natural as the 'rites of spring', and therefore impossible to challenge.

The adulation and exaltation of male sporting heroes focuses public approval on certain sanctioned styles of masculine behaviour which become powerful and all-pervasive. The masculine styles of our male sporting heroes create a structure of dominance in the gender order as a whole, which puts the culturally idealised forms of masculine character that our sporting heroes represent at the top of the hierarchy.

Many men as they grow older, however, tire of the pressures of club life, and react against the team, rejecting team sports in favour of more individual pursuits with anarchistic or iconoclastic appeal. But the impression of escape from the strictures of the team and club may be illusory, even if the sport chosen is as resolutely unconventional as climbing.

Junk Male

THE ENDLESS TEST

The site of the activity of climbing is related to other sites of masculinisation; it is separate and distinct from daily life, and is generally difficult of access. A certain degree of strength and competence is required merely to get to the foot of a major climb, let alone do it. In the case of major mountains in ranges such as the Himalayas, access can be even more difficult, necessitating a long approach march, which is of great social significance to the members of the climbing team. They may not know each other, and the march will help them to settle into their roles and places in the expedition.

In the monochromatic rock and ice world of high-altitude climbing it might be said that the climber undergoes a mild form of sensory deprivation; many climbers remark on their return to inhabited areas that seeing such things as a flower or their first child occasions unexpectedly deep emotional responses. At the very least, climbing is a retreat into a harsh, austere and ascetic world, devoid of distractions such as women.

Climbing is a paradoxical sport. One person, encumbered with rope and various means to attach that rope to the rock as they progress, sets off up a face. The second remains behind at the foot of the rock. Should the first person — the leader — fall, the second person is the one who stops that fall from being in all probability fatal, providing the leader has placed sufficiently good protection on the route. But should the leader find himself assailed by fear, or faced with a move of such difficulty that he will be unlikely to achieve it successfully, the second can do absolutely nothing.

> There was a line of cracks stretching across a steep wall in between us and the sky line. Guarding any entrance to them

was an enormous flake. It was angular and about ten feet across, and it was possible to see light behind it in places. It seemed to be glued to the side of the mountain by a few patches of ice. Wearing my crampons, I front-pointed up to it and thumped it hard with my hammer. BOOMM! it replied threateningly.

'What do you think to this, Joe, do you think it'll be safe? It might skate off with me riding it.'

'Oh, it'll be alright,' he replied. 'It must have been there long enough. Anyway,' he added reassuringly, 'it's not my lead, is it?'[1]

A climber is completely alone as he leads, even though his second may be able to see him and talk with him. Having confidence, no matter how illusory, in his abilities and gear and the close attention of the second to paying out the rope, the leader climbs silently upward.

The rite or test in climbing is a deeply personal one; it is the overcoming of fear. In climbing there is a good chance of a fall, especially if you are 'pushing your grades', that is, trying to climb as well as you can or better. Facing the vertigo, the dizzying void with all its threat and invitation, is the test for the climber. This test is most clearly encountered at one point on a climb, the crux. This is the hardest move or sequence of moves on that climb, which probably give it its grading of difficulty and particular character. The combination of fear and physical difficulty that make climbing can best be experienced on the crux of a climb.

David Craig, an English climbing writer, has talked of the 'fear barrier', which he sees as a 'kind of absurd negative charge' which gathers round the crux of a climb and scatters a climber's mental clarity.[2]

> The fear barrier is a zone of nothing, where you cannot be. As you move up closer to it, it may enter into you — you become nothing, your strength is cancelled, weakness hollows out your arms, your feet can't be trusted, your brain ceases to screen clear images, your balance shakes out of true, your imagination can't conceive of a way beyond. But if the fear barrier fails to invade you, it cancels itself, and you remain yourself, strong, limber, and collected, in a fit state to savour the lovely jubilation that floods through you as you move on and up, unscathed.[3]

The words 'you become nothing' indicate the effect of the test if failed: the self is destroyed. Climbing therefore is a typically male activity, because it is about retaining control of the self. The self must be held together by the exercise of will, or the climber will fail and fall.

In looking at what is gained by overcoming a crux or a complete climb, it is worth looking at what climbers have said after a climb. A first ascent is a particularly hard one; there is no guidebook with a summary of the route and helpful hints about technique. You are merely pushing out into the unknown, seeking the point where the impossible becomes the merely improbable. One famous English climber, in talking of a particularly difficult first ascent, said that 'when we'd done it, we just sat here, Bert and me. We didn't say a word. We were so . . . used — full — happy — contented — knackered'.[4] To consider this mixture of emotions is to see that the climber is talking about the calm inner confidence and equilibrium that follows a test which has been met and overcome. Such an effect is, however, fleeting. It is not enough that a climber may test himself once; he must go on and on testing himself, thus showing yet again that masculinity is never finally proved, but is always open to question and the need for confirmation.

Concluding his comments on the 'fear barrier', David Craig goes on to make the interesting comment that the 'perfectly integrated person would not need to keep proving himself', yet he knows, like so many other climbers, that 'as soon as the last climb that fired me has died down to a gentle glow, I have to be out there attempting the seemingly infinite series of routes I have been setting myself in the meantime'.[5] So in climbing, as in so many other male activities, constant repetition is necessary to confirm the self as masculine.

It is worth considering the way in which competition works in climbing. For a climber in the middle grades there will always be enough climbs to test him, but consider the leading rock-climber at the very limit of the sport: he must, it is true, look within himself and test himself there, but each new route that he puts up becomes a challenge to the nerve, the masculinity of the climbers who then try to repeat that route, and with whom he is therefore in implicit competition.

COMPETITION

The site of the rite, the route, can therefore become a medium of competition between climbers. In this way one can compare oneself even with climbers from the past. A route can also become a challenge thrown out by the leader of the team to his or her second, for it follows that no climbers who climb together can be too different in their abilities, or they would not be able to climb as a team. If one is clearly better than the other, then the other could not follow their leads, as the cruxes or the route itself would be altogether too hard for them to follow. This leads

Junk Male

to a certain smug superiority when a climber can say he 'watched seconds [that is, people following him on a rope] struggling up something difficult that I had led'.[6] Another practice that emerges in such situations is known as sandbagging. This is when a climber new to a cliff is casually directed by local climbers towards a very hard route on which he is likely to fail and fall, for the sake of the amusement of the locals. Here is a description of just such an event at Kangaroo Point, a Brisbane rock-climbing venue.

> [H]aving successfully sandbagged a victim who is about to set off up a line of never-tested bolts and drooping pegs without the benefit of ten top-ropings [in climbing jargon, to attempt a very hard and poorly protected route, one on which the leader is likely to become frightened and fall] the locals can scarcely contain their glee and begin to dance and giggle in such a covert fashion that the sandbaggee becomes suspicious. Lots of useless advice and errors of omission usually induce the desired screaming winger [fall]. The sandbaggers fall about on the grass [at the foot of the climb] in hysterics . . . and the gullible foreigner hangs limply, too exhausted to complain.[7]

All this may explain why male climbers have reacted so uniformly negatively to the presence of competitive women climbers on the climbing scene. The Australian outdoors magazine *Wild* had to apologise on one occasion for offensive comment on the climbing of women. The incident is illustrative of the challenge that men feel in climbing. In the Grampians there is a climb called, evocatively enough, 'Passport to Insanity'. This climb was first done by mechanical aids and graded at 26 by two men. (Grades are numerical: technical

Sport

climbing starts at about 8, and goes from there in ascending order of difficulty to about 30, though the scale is open-ended.)

So confident were the first climbers of the route that it would not be repeated, or if repeated, it would not be climbed 'free' (that is, without the mechanical aids), that they left a jar on the lip of the huge overhang that formed the crux of the climb, with a promissory note that any person who free-climbed the route would get $500 from them. Some time later a woman climber, Nyrie Dodd, did the climb, and found the jar, and she had done the climb free of any mechanical aids. In a copy of *Wild*'s companion publication *Rock*, a cartoon was published which implied that Nyrie Dodd and Louise Shepherd, who had seconded Dodd on the ascent, were engaged in a lesbian relationship, and at a later date *Wild* published an apology for the cartoon.[8] Dodd and Shepherd had trespassed, literally and figuratively, on male terrain, and so were to be attacked for their presumption. No wonder Shepherd had titled an earlier article for *Rock* 'Sex 'n' Jugs [climbing jargon for 'a good hold' as much as slang for 'breasts'] 'n' Rock 'n' Role'[*sic*].[9]

LANGUAGE AND ITS PURPOSE

Something needs to be said at this point about the nature and purpose of language used between men compared to its nature and purpose between women. One Australian woman writer has said of conversations between women friends that

> their themes are often repetitive, like all good music; there are minor keys, variations, trills and flourishes. Lento, presto, piano, forte. Women make this music out of their daily lives, their shrewd understanding. Women colour themselves in, and

their friends and their lovers, endlessly; women make their reality of the subtlest shades of colour and sound.[10]

Women seem to use language to create links, and draw the colours of emotion from each other.

Male conversation, on the other hand, seems to be about denying links, separation and alienation. One chief form of male conversation is banter. Banter is based on 'every kind of irony, sarcasm, pun and cliched reply', and so may sound to the casual listener to be purely 'aggressive, a form in which the masculine ego asserts itself'. However, the operation of banter is far more complex than that. The nature of banter among a group of men, which 'depends on a close intimate and personal understanding of the person who is the butt of attack' means that such exchanges are a 'way of affirming the bond of love between men while appearing to deny it'.[11] So male banter is about getting close to another man or men, but not too close; like the similar poles of a magnet when pushed towards each other, the closer the proximity, the greater the pushing away. The various methods of humour used are an attempt to deny close and serious bonding, to prevent the creation of any really profound emotional link between the men in the circle of the conversation.

The dominance of banter in communication between men can be a source of frustration and even despair for a man when he tries to seek out real support from his close men friends. The same irony, sarcasm, pun, innuendo and word-play that seemed previously to promise so much solidarity suddenly become the very means by which an attempt to draw on or create any real rapport within the group is deflected, defused, or even derided. The humour, which appears to act as a real link between members of the group, keeps feeling at arm's length; so few genuine affective links are formed between men. (There is also an underlying element of homophobia in this, but that will be discussed elsewhere.) Once a male has realised that he cannot draw on the group for support, he discovers his fundamentally solitary situation. No wonder men turn to women for the colour they provide in their overt and easy discussion of the emotional content in their lives.

Banter has relevance to the world of climbing because it is virtually an all-male world. Men choose to climb, and separate themselves into all-male groups far from female company. As one climber has brutally put it, 'girls were for necking [heavy petting] and hops [dances]'.[12] Despite men putting themselves in a situation where some real interaction might take place, the nature of banter means that there is a slight but significant distance created and maintained, and real communion, the opening up of one man to another, is denied.

In order to demonstrate the nature of banter I will discuss several examples from the approaches and ascents of some Himalayan peaks. Any major Himalayan climb will have a long approach walk, sometimes lasting several days or more. During this walk roles will be taken up and the status of individual members established, and groups begin to form within the expedition as a whole. Peter Boardman, an experienced Himalayan climber, commented on the walk-in of one expedition that 'conversations ... had all the cut, thrust and parry of a sword fight as we tried to penetrate the armour of each other's pretence'.[13] Anyone is fair game in an attempt to lower their status through ridicule:

> I was toiling up a steep and muddy path behind John. He came across a snake, sleeping on the path, and quickly flicked

it at me with his umbrella. The snake wrapped around my leg and I danced about until I had shaken it clear. I was furious, and hit John as hard as I could with my ski-stick.

'There're poisonous pit vipers around here.'

'It wasn't poisonous, I could tell from its mouth,' said Guy [another member of the expedition].

'My last trip was nearly ruined by thoughtlessness like that,' I yelled. 'How, how . . .' I searched for the epithet . . . 'how childish, how unprofessional.'

The others snorted with laughter as I stalked off, sulking for over an hour. I did not play the hypochondriac again.[14]

Sometimes conversation merely becomes a string of insults:

'Watch that rope, Pete, you're supposed to be a professional guide.'

'Shut up, you middle-aged hippie.'

'You're a middle-class achiever.'

'Working-class hero.'[15]

Competition also reveals itself on the mountain. Fear is ever-present, but must never be admitted. As Peter Boardman and Joe Tasker lie awake in a tent in a camp at night, the following exchange takes place:

Back at Camp 1 in the evening Joe and I were lying, wide awake and twitching, listening to the avalanches.

'You know on Everest Camp 2 was hit by the blast of an avalanche which threw a tent in the air with five people in it on top of another one,' I said.

'Once hit, twice shy.'

Sport

'We're right at the end of the run-out for those seracs [tall ice columns that may collapse, thus starting an avalanche] on Twins Peak. They would pick up a hell of a speed falling two thousand feet.'

'Well, there's nothing we can do about it. Anyway, we can identify the shell noises.'

I started up at the first thumping of blocks.

'A trial run,' said Joe. 'It takes two aims for them to line up the target, and then . . .'

'Who's the spotter then? God?'[16]

In this brief exchange the speaker feels fear, and feels that he has lost the encounter, as his comments reveal fear, while his partner's do not. The use of humour here is to simultaneously distance and control fear, to distance the other person, and to maintain status.

The emotional content of climbing is by its nature difficult to convey. Climbers themselves have evolved a particularly male mode of talking when recounting their adventures, that of understatement. This in itself, though, can be taken so far that it also becomes a pose. An example of understatement is a description by Eric Shipton of a potentially fatal moment in the Himalayas. His companion had fallen down one side of a knife-edged ridge, and Shipton had to jump off the ridge the other way in order to act as a counterweight. Speaking of this at a lecture, he looked at his audience 'from his lean height, out of scooped eye-sockets [and] said in his extremely slow, quiet, stainless steel voice, "It was . . . quite an . . . alarming . . . moment".'[17]

Related to banter and understatement is that uniquely male activity which was called 'line-shooting' but has since come to be known as 'bull-shitting', and its opposed art, 'taking the

Junk Male

piss'. 'Line-shooting' and 'bull-shitting' are essentially an attempt by one male to convince another male of the truth of a story or a position, no matter how improbable or far-fetched it may sound, for there is a considerable element of bluff in the game. 'Taking the piss' is the art of attacking the pretensions expressed by the line-shooter or bull-shitter. One climber, talking of his early days as a climber, said that he

> soon learned, for example, the strategies of the climber's real art, known as 'taking the piss', which is probably the most important form of protection in a climber's repertoire. We learned to take swift and ruthless advantage of any misfortune, particularly if someone had nosedived off a climb, or, better still, was just about to, to be especially inhumane where relations with a woman were concerned and once a crack in the armour had been exposed to exploit it mercilessly.[18]

This brief statement encapsulates the climber's mode of discourse, and also hints at the sexism underlying it.

CLIMBING AS METAPHOR FOR MASCULINE BEHAVIOUR

I would like to focus on two climbers and one ascent in particular in order to demonstrate the ways in which climbing shows typical male behaviour that associates it with other sporting settings and masculine behaviours. The two men were Pete Boardman and Joe Tasker, and the ascent was of Changabang, a 22 500-foot (6858-metre) mountain in the Garwhal in Northern India. Joe Tasker and Pete Boardman were above all a successful team; they combined, within a larger expedition or as a pair, to achieve a number of difficult ascents,

Sport

and their climbing relationship spanned a number of years. Sadly they were both killed in an attempt on the South West Ridge of Everest, when they set off to climb one of the last remaining unclimbed lines on that mountain.

In looking at the experience of the pair in climbing Changabang, I would like to focus on four aspects of that expedition. The first is the nature of the communication between them, and what it reveals about men and dialogue between them. The second is the nature of teamwork revealed under the stress of climbing. The third is the nature of the will in climbing, and this is a particularly male quality. Lastly I would like to discuss the experience of a climb, as a whole, as a metaphor for male relationships, and what this reveals about men getting closer to other men.

When Pete Boardman and Joe Tasker started working together towards the climb, they 'often engaged in gibing sessions with each other which often caused people to wonder that we should be going on an expedition together'.[19] However, once the climb has begun the nature of their conversation becomes different:

It was a game.
  'Are your feet cold, Joe?'
  'No, are yours?'
  'Oh no, it's just that my lace has come undone.'[20]

This game was maintained so that in the end 'neither of us ever opened up completely'.[21]

As the climb continued, 'conversation ... died to a minimum',[22] but this did not mean an end to concern for the other. The other became a double, assumed to be feeling the same:

> I was much more physically or hygienically aware than I had been on previous expeditions. I was carefully changing my underwear, washing and combing my hair and cleaning my teeth and keeping warm and comfortable. I was constantly checking my pulse rate, to gauge my fitness and state of acclimatisation. I knew that Joe would feel hopelessly let down if something simple, but damning, happened to me. I wondered if he felt the same.[23]

Or the other could be an opposite, a foil to emotion, and a corrective to subjectivity:

> I stopped, gasping with the load, and looked up at Joe, wondering what he was thinking, what motivated him. Perhaps I was just being over-dramatic, too subjective, and Joe was feeling calm, objective and factual.[24]

Despite these vague wonderings, nothing is ever done to overcome the barriers against real contact. This may be because there was a perception by them both that 'if we opened up our relationship whilst on the climb, the mountain might exploit our weaknesses. We must present a united front against the mountain and swallow the subtleties of interaction'.[25]

Even at the summit, where it might be thought that there was reason and occasion for some display and sharing of emotion, their separateness remains:

> I thought we would at least shake hands, but Joe did not make any gestures. I wondered if he felt he had just done another climb and that life would go on until he did the next one. Perhaps wiser than I, he had already started focussing his

> concentration on the problems we were to face on the descent
> — perhaps to touch each other would have broken the spell
> of our separateness.[26]

Even though they have chosen to climb with each other, spent nearly two months not more than a rope's length — about a hundred and fifty feet (58 metres) apart — they cannot overcome the distance between them as men.

The lack of real communication does not seem to have damaged or prevented a very real teamwork emerging in their climbing. Even though it is not explicitly discussed, each begins to feel a growing confidence about the climb. 'Without stopping to talk about it, by some imperceptible transition of thought, it was clear that we could climb the West Wall.'[27] The two climbers 'had generated such unified intensity of purpose that whatever Joe said I had been thinking at the same time'.[28] Their strength of belief in themselves was so great that it took on a separate benevolent existence around them; 'our combined abilities seemed to have made a third, invisible quality outside ourselves, in which we had implicit faith.'[29]

But tensions between the two climbers could easily surface. One afternoon on an ice-field, Joe Tasker was ahead of Pete Boardman and taking pictures of him. Boardman, who was affected by the altitude, was taking occasional rests by leaning his head on his forearm, when he noticed Tasker photographing him in that 'controversial resting position' as the photograph is captioned in *The Shining Mountain*. It is significant that Boardman has heard of Tasker's photographs of his partner on a previous climb, which showed that climber 'collapsed, flat on his back, on the summit ridge'.[30] Boardman 'gasped as loudly as I could, "If you take another picture like that, I'll thump you."'[31]

Two conventions have simultaneously been broken. The first is the convention against direct statement of feeling. As Tasker commented in his diary:

> [I]t is true that we were on edge, but it amazed me that his anger should be so close to the surface. Under stress there are always a thousand assumed reasons for losing one's temper, but in one's mind it is clear that they are only the product of circumstances and one holds back.[32]

Boardman had failed to hold back, and the effect of his outburst is that he has 'lost respect'.[33]

Tasker observed later in his own account of the incident in *Savage Arena* that the 'fragile, often begrudging rapport which had held us together was for me destroyed; a sense of aimlessness and futility overwhelmed me; we were both far apart however well we had done so far with the climb'.[34] Again, distance is emphasised.

The second convention that has been broken is that of showing the effort of climbing. Any image that shows a climber actually suffering is against the unwritten convention concerning the representation of the activity. Only the relaxed or powerful pose can be shown, not the vulnerable. High-altitude climbers may gasp from the rarefied air, they may double over, coughing painfully, they may stop in their tracks, unable to take a step for a few minutes at a time, but these things are never shown. All that is seen are the images of smooth, impenetrable power and effective action.

The nature of climbing does involve the use of will; often it is the will alone that drives a cringing, reluctant body upwards over difficult ground, into dangerous situations towards a goal.

Sport

In climbing a major mountain rather than a single-pitch rock climb, the summit becomes a solid and specific goal. Superb climbing done on a route is of not much status if the summit is not achieved. The 'unified intensity of purpose' generated by Boardman and Tasker indicates a healthy level of determination, but even Boardman can comment that 'obsession is always a danger for a mountaineer',[35] for while on a climb it is possible that a climber will lose proportion and put the summit before rational consideration of weather, objective danger such as rockfall and the possibility of avalanche, or put the summit before even life itself. Boardman can say 'the steady pressure of risk, that had forced us into being alert for weeks, had generated an intensity that, during moments of reflection, was frightening'.[36] At such moments he becomes a 'prisoner of [his] own ambition'.[37] This particularly male focus on a goal to the exclusion of considerations of life and sanity may lead to many climbing accidents, as desire for the summit overrides common sense. Speaking of a disastrous season on K2, the world's second-highest mountain, Jim Curran, an experienced commentator on mountaineering, can say of six of the twelve deaths that occurred in 1986

> there was, in my opinion, an element of 'the last throw of the dice' at work. I believe all of them saw climbing K2 as the crowning moment of their Himalayan careers. Failure would be difficult to contemplate, and harder to accept. It does seem to me that over-ambition played a significant part in some of the disasters.[38]

Lastly, the idea of climbing, especially mountaineering on major peaks, as a metaphor. We see how in rock climbing or in attempts on major Himalayan peaks the men band together into a team, and then set themselves apart from others in order to submit themselves to a shared test. If some real exchange of insight and experience occurred during the climb, and real emotional ties were formed between the members of the team, then indeed climbing might be an idyllic sport, one in which the usual subtle demarcations that hold men apart were overcome. However, it seems from the preceding discussion that it is not; even when men remove themselves from the daily round, their underlying codes of separation and competition rule, and no real affective bonds are formed.

While the nature of the activity — men forming a group and sharing in intense effort in pursuit of a peak experience — is a distinctly sexual one, it seems that no real communion takes place. Once again the experience of men is barren and solitary. While it is difficult for me to admit this, as I chose to climb in the belief that it was not like other sports, or rather that it was not played in the same way, I now have to admit that climbing is also dominated by the same limited parameters of masculine behaviour that were so clearly apparent in other team games, whether on the field or in the bar. In the mountains there are no carefully marked white lines, no umpires blowing whistles, but one's behaviour as a man is just as rigidly determined.

OTHER MEN

It's great having a lot of mates, but that's all they are — mates! If I didn't follow the crowd, I'd love to see how many mates I'd have then ... Well, look at me. I've got six brothers, I'm a member of a football team, and I'm bored silly.

Seventeen-year-old boy, writing in his exam paper

I couldn't change [my homosexual ways] but I might change my image. From now on I would allow nothing in my manner or appearance to betray my affliction ... I would buy a tweed sports coat, a pair of brogue shoes, I would become a rugby referee, grow a moustache and abandon cigarettes in favour of a pipe.

Garry Wotherspoon, *City of the Plain*

Homosociality and homophobia

Other men confront us with difficult choices. In our adolescence and youth we crave their company and approval, for they can confirm our heterosexual gender identity as men in ways that women cannot. When we later desert our male 'mates' to pursue other demanding callings such as marriage and parenting, we must do so in spite of the rejection of such activities by the emotionally closed bachelor world. It is only after some time away from it that we can see the homosocial world of the sports club, the pub and sometimes even the workplace as being limited in its horizons and emotionally impoverished. We have to move out in order to move on.

However, in making the effort to link with others, the women and children in our lives especially, we sometimes feel the unsettling undertow of old allegiances and loyalties. We don't notice how other men mesh with us, through the masonic handshake of masculinity to which we unquestioningly respond, until women remind us of an appreciation of their rights and importance.

Similarly, gay men challenge us to include them in our patterns of friendship. Our heterosexuality is founded on a visceral rejection of any attempt by other men to get really close to us, for while our masculinity means that occasionally we feel the need to be homosocial, it is also predicated on the exclusion of the homosexual. So the cost of our identification with other men is our rejection of other more real and sexual ways of dealing with them, and the creation of a hierarchy of sexual behaviours which sees some as stigmatised and others as acceptable. The experiences of gay men are of interest and value, yet society acts to marginalise them as a group whose sexuality is too problematical to be assimilated into the mainstream of sexual practice.

The experience of many Australian men is still chiefly homosocial, and I will look at the edges of such experience when men look at men with desire and what happens to interaction at that moment. I will also look at the dilemmas that other men present when it comes to standing against masculine practice. Throughout this chapter the common contradictory forces that make men group together, yet also keep them apart, are homophobia, a very common stance for Australian men, and homosociality, the tendency of men to seek comfort and reinforcement through same-sex social settings.

When men begin to come to terms with their need for real and close bonding with men, they will have to confront that particular closet that all straight men have: their attitude to other men and how they would respond if other men's sexuality was directed at them. Then they may realise, as Martin Amis admitted, that 'I knew nothing about homosexuality . . . I had never registered the otherness'[1] of homosexual desire. Heterosexuality is founded on the rejection of the erotic and social attraction of men by men in favour of women. And yet other men are those with whom we share the most experience and understanding. But even so there are clearly finite limits to straight men's experience and knowledge, and they would be wrong to think, along with many other puzzled men, that 'homosexuality [is] a version of heterosexuality. It is something else again'.[2]

Other Men

Once men subject their heterosexuality to a deep questioning they might find the same insight as gay men when forced to confront the hopes that those around them had for their 'successful' or 'normal' development into a replication of their sexuality and lifestyle. For the dominance of heterosexuality is 'based on an illusion, on the idea that our society runs on heterosexual romance. [It is] everyone's concern to keep this merry-go-round going. But it only takes one person to get off to stop this continuing myth'.[3] Once a gay man has stepped outside heterosexual masculinity, he can take 'an ironical approach to social institutions, because oppressed people can't take seriously the institutions more socially integrated people do'[4] as Ian McNeill, a Sydney gay writer, has commented.

Looking back at the history of Australia, buggery arrived in Botany Bay along with the First Fleet. Estimates of the amount of homosexual activity in the colony's early days vary. After close research into the behaviour of prisoners on Norfolk Island, where up to six hundred convicts were held at any one time, Robert Hughes concludes with a question: 'Once a decade, or sixty times a day?'[5] Contemporary sources give a sobering picture. To arrive on Norfolk Island, according to one observer, meant that hardened criminals and first offenders alike 'are immediately on their disembarkation thrust amongst the veriest monsters of crime, from the cold-blooded murderer trebly convicted, to the wretch whose enormity Blackstone [the English legal authority] characterises as "Inter Christianos non nominandum"'.[6] Such tortured euphemism and the use of Latin tags characterise early descriptions of such practices.

Not surprisingly in an all-male social environment, the convicts turned to each other for social and perhaps sexual solace. Robert Stuart Pringle, a convict department magistrate, mentions some convict couples who characterised themselves as 'man and wife', and who could not bear to be parted, and who 'manifest as much eager earnestness for the society of each other as members of the opposite sex'.[7] The Australian male's homosociality, where men choose the company of their own sex over the opposite, may be seen to have its origins in such an environment of necessity.

Even at such a delicate stage in the formation of a nation's sexual identity, the notion that such activity might have been caused by the convicts being sent away together was actively avoided by those who had sent them. Robert Stuart Pringle, the magistrate mentioned above, wrote a Report for the Houses of Parliament in 1847, but all references to homosexual practices were deleted before printing. As a modern historian of gay Australian life has commented, this means that 'a whole range of materials usually available to the historian — diaries, and letters, and memoirs — have simply not been available'.[8]

Homosociality was at the very heart of settled life in Australia. The pairs of convict stock-keepers, for example, isolated for weeks at a time, experienced the 'pair bonding, the feeling of reliance on one's "mate", that would lie for ever at the heart of masculine social behaviour in Australia'.[9] But homosociality as a norm for male behaviour does not mean that sexual expression between males is seen as positive. Australian cultural icons must be free of the taint of homosexuality. Those writers who cover the myth of mateship among the Diggers of the First World War, for example, are very keen to point out that the feelings the soldiers had for their martial 'mates' were not homosexual in nature. One such writer notes:

Other Men

On Anzac eve the Melbourne *Age* published an article in which it was stated that this special thing was, in fact, sublimated homosexuality. Surely there can be no greater evidence of the inability of any who were not with them to understand the relationship that these men knew.[10]

The writer seems unusually moved to reject an element of homosexuality in war-based friendship. The Digger, like all central male icons in Australia, must be heterosexual.

Maintaining heterosexual identity

The horror at submerged homosexuality is perhaps because a deep and uninspected sentimentality towards other men underlies much of male interaction. There are many occasions on which prominent public display of male-to-male contact is possible, contact which might under other circumstances be construed as a slur on the assumed heterosexuality of the men involved, and be likely to trigger a violent response. One such setting is the game of Australian Rules football. Players pat each other's buttocks, embrace, kiss, walk arm-in-arm, and look at each other with frankly admiring eyes, behaviour which under other circumstances might elicit aggressive responses.

It is worth considering examples of the appearance of homosexual impulses at moments other than the publicly sanctioned. One of those moments occurs in Paul Radley's novel *Best Mates*, as Mitch and Chid are recovering from an encounter with a voracious nurse:

> Mitch cleaned up while Chid got back into his own cot. When he finished he went to give Chid a Nickie [his

> wife]-like goodnight hug, but Chid turned away defensively. Then, watching Mitch get sadly back into his bunk in the shadowed night light, he said affectionately, 'Let's not get too affectionate.'
>
> 'You're right.'[11]

Despite the presence of alcohol and the relaxed mood of post-coital exchange, the seething, powerful feeling latent in the occasion cannot be fully called up. It is as if the heterosexual Australian male can let his one special friend come close to him, but not too close. While male-to-male bonding is one of the prerequisites for masculine identity in Australia, if that bonding is too close it destroys heterosexual identity, because it leads to homosexual identity. So men must gather, but not too closely. The social siting of man to man in most situations will mean that this tension between acceptance and encouragement and rejection and shunning is not felt. However, if it is experienced or perceived, then it may lead to explosive violence, because the sexuality of the male who is moved against is perceived as more totally compromised and threatened than it could ever be by any female action.

The level of violence with which a heterosexual man is prepared to defend his gender identity from another male points to another unacknowledged heterosexual male anxiety: anal penetration. For heterosexual men homosex is associated with anal intercourse, now doubly horrifying in the post-AIDS age, and so the hysterical abhorrence with which homosex is treated derives from a dimly perceived memory of anal vulnerability. Men tend to forget that the male anus is the most staunchly defended orifice of the human body, far more rigorously defended than the female vagina or anus. The penalties for anal invasion of the male body have historically always been greater than the penalties for equivalent invasion of the female body.

HOMOSEXUALITY IN THE AUSTRALIAN LITERARY TRADITION

One context in which the marginalisation of gay experience is particularly clear is in the recent literary history of Australia. In their work on the emerging range of writing in Australia in the late 1980s, *The New Diversity*, Ken Gelder and Paul Salzman seem less confident in talking about male homosex than they do talking of either heterosex, feminist representations of heterosex or lesbian sex. While they feel able to confidently define a 'lesbian novel',[12] they are far more tentative in talking about gay themes. A contentious conclusion to explain the relative prominence of lesbian writing is that it has 'had a respected place in feminist discourse ... [because] ... lesbian sexuality is construed as a far more positive force than male sexuality'.[13] Certainly, after a burst of heterosexual literary activity by Frank Moorhouse and Michael Wilding in the late sixties and early seventies, heterosex has been less prominent. A literary quarterly like *Meanjin* has had no fiction depicting heterosex since 1986, and yet in that time a number of stories by women have appeared in its pages in which lesbian sex has been portrayed in a favourable light, though there have been no depictions in that period of male homosex.

Two writers who bury gay content in more complex, layered novels are Randolph Stow and David Malouf. Randolph Stow's semi-autobiographical *The Merry-Go-Round in the Sea* is a substantial work which explores the experience of a country boy as he passes from a naive provincial life to a more mature

Junk Male

view of the world on the threshold of a doubtful maturity. The novel gains immensely from its restraint in portraying the central relationship between the young protagonist and an adored older male, which is never consummated except in such a way as to guarantee its collapse:

> The road was going through a yellow stubble field, like a courtyard between walls of grey-green scrub.
> 'We're being pretty honest with each other,' Rick said. 'You love me, don't you, Rob?'
> 'No,' said the boy, bitterly. 'Not if you're going to leave me to grow up all by myself.'
> He kicked the mare, and plunged away, cantering and then galloping through the stubble, beside the whizzing scrub.[14]

Similarly David Malouf's novel *Johnno* deals with a relationship between the bookish narrator Dante, a cautious middle-class boy who turns into a writer, and the larrikin, extroverted, iconoclastic rebel of the title. Johnno leaves Brisbane to rid himself of Australia, while the timid Dante remains there to grow old but not up, and Johnno sends various invitations to Dante to join him or write to him at various exotic locales around the world. At the novel's end, Johnno is drowned in an accident which seems a suicide, and his last words to Dante in a letter are similar in mood to the belated admission and recognition of love in Stow's novel:

> I've spent years writing letters to you and you never answer, even when you write back. I've loved you — and you've never given a fuck for me, except as a character in one of your funny stories.[15]

Other Men

The novel's mood is, like Stow's novel, also fuelled by a tension of distance between the narrator and Johnno, and significantly the strong affection they feel is never acknowledged or given form.

The caution with which homosexual themes and content are treated in Australia is a reflection of a deep-seated reticence about the validity of such experiences and views on the part of those who hold them and live them, as well as by an essentially unsympathetic literary setting. An exception to this rule is Sasha Soldatow's *Private — Do Not Open*. The book is unusual in that it was published by a major press and deals directly with gay subject matter and sexual behaviour. Not only that, but the narratorial stances are crude and confrontational. This somehow works against the acceptance of such ideas and content. The very vehemence of the tone of the book mitigates against its assimilation by critics and readers. The text lacks the more relaxed tone which might make it possible for an uninvolved and differently aligned reader to accept.

Another exception to this reticence is the graphic description of casual gay sex which opens Frank Moorhouse's short story 'The Everlasting Secret Family':

> He moves his head for me to follow and I do at a distance, like a dog, the wordless animal knowingness of male gutter sex.
>
> I follow him, he taking me I suppose at first to his room, but then it becomes clear that he is looking for any place, a doorway, a porch, an alley. We come to a church. He walks into a path at the side of the church and stands there.
>
> I follow him the submissive dog. He does not speak but simply unzips himself. I kneel before him, burrow in with my fingers and pull out the soft, erecting penis and take it into my mouth.

Junk Male

> I am taken down into that self-contained black world where there is no other thing, feeling, or sound but a moist, hot penis and my yielding mouth. There is nothing in the world for that time but his penis moving towards its explosion and my mouth moving, shaping, and pulling and wanting it. The mouth that is saying without words, yes, come, use me, fill me. No outside world existing, no other reward, no other way of being.
>
> Holding his balls, drawing out his sperm, he grunts, his only sound, a giving grunt and then the pulsing sperm, the completed link, the joining by the highest sensation and the most brawny of fluids, two strangers in a path beside a church.
>
> He pulls himself away, he zips himself, and he steps around me, walking away. Not a word, no gesture, no sign.
>
> That was right and how it should be.[16]

The story in which the above occurs is the one that gives the anthology its name, and yet it is buried at the back of the book.

Gay fiction is published and survives when it nests within a larger work in the overall masculine and heterosexist tradition. Thus David Malouf's first story in his collection *Antipodes*, 'Southern Skies', is a story of an adolescent boy's sexual awakening by an older person. In this case, however, an unusual conclusion is allowed; the boy rejects the older woman's advances allowing himself instead to be seduced by the older man. The story is of teenage narrator who is at a sexually androgynous stage of psychological development; the boy is torn between the life of the head and the life of the body, the life of books and the body: 'I see myself as a kind of centaur, half-boy, half-bike, forever wheeling down suburban streets under the poincianas, on my way to football practice or the library.'[17] The boy has a superabundance of undefined energy which might rush in any direction at any moment, and this energy is tied to his emerging sexuality; he is '. . . half-boy, half-bike, half aimless energy and half a machine that could hurtle off at a moment's notice in any one of a hundred directions'.[18]

In the end the direction the boy chooses, or allows, is to be initiated into the mysteries by the older man who is regarded as a 'caricature of a man' by the narrator's friends. Though not explicitly stated, it seems that the incident of the boy's sexual fondling at the older man's phallic telescope, during which the boy experiences himself 'from out there, as just a figure with his eye to the lens . . .',[19] will define the pattern of his subsequent sexual life, and so a choice has been made which overturns the usual happy induction of the narrator into heterosexuality through a sexual experiment with an older woman.

To say that explicit depiction of gay sex disqualifies a work from acceptance is perhaps to fall into the trap of wishing to avoid contemplating the very differences of sexual activity that constitute the otherness of the gay man. If readers are able to overlook specific sexual practice because it is left vague, then they may substitute their own, thus safely sentimentalising the situation. And such sentimentality, of the 'but really they are just like us' kind, is just what writers such as Soldatow seek to confront and destroy.

However, such novels as Alan Hollinghurst's *The Swimming Pool Library* and Edmund White's *Boy's Own Story* portray homosex with an absence of insistence, and a directness that seems to encourage its consideration in addition to their novels' many other strengths. By contrast the inclusion of homosexual content, or even undertones of homosexuality, seems to confuse and mystify Australian critics. Speaking of David Malouf's *Johnno*, one commentator says 'that [the central] friendship might have a sexual dimension obviously reflects a general reluctance to deal with homosexual overtones in fiction . . . even when . . . the subject becomes unavoidable'.[20] Many reviewers of Soldatow's *Private — Do Not Open* openly included clear statements of their difference in their reviews, to at once declare their distance and qualify their comment.

Certainly it is true that while there is no significant body of gay fiction — that is, fiction that deals openly and directly with gay male experience — the rest of Australia will have to put up with the stereotypes that have been created and recycled through the media and popular culture, though comings out by people such as Patrick White in his autobiographical *Flaws in the Glass* and Stuart Challender, the Melbourne conductor, should play a 'significant part in altering stereotypical perceptions of homosexuality'.[21] Such fiction might help other men to understand the different voltage of gay life.

BONDING OR ESTRANGEMENT — A BALANCING ACT

In an analysis of hegemonic masculinity from a heterosexual man's viewpoint, there is a danger of coming to regard the gay man as a person who has successfully overcome masculinisation and taken off in pursuit of a new mode of being male. To say this is to make gay men the white knights and standard-bearers of the belated charge by heterosexual men intent on challenging masculinity.

The heterosexism of many analyses of hegemonic masculinity shows when it comes to considering relationships between men, whether gay or straight, for we

Other Men

> have to choose between a vision of the world in which [heterosexual] men are more sensitive and human but are still the 'real' men at the top of the social order, and a radically new vision that entails the transformation of masculinity and sexuality and the challenging of other forms of domination.[22]

Any analysis of masculinity must include not only the way men and women interact and how patterns of dominance have been established there, but also the ways in which men interact with men, and how some kinds of men are marginalised and disadvantaged in the process.

Many men who have set out on the path of self-analysis have found themselves lonely, not because they do not get on well with women; on the contrary, their self-distrust and self-loathing, their caution and guilt will probably allow them to get on better with feminised women who hold them in thrall because they speak the language that will tap into those emotions. Such men will find themselves lonely because they will, perhaps without even noticing it, change their lives in order to avoid contact with men whose views and attitudes they find offensive. If men, however, need other men to feel validated, and validated in ways that the company of women cannot replace, then they will feel a vague sense of unease when such validation is removed. For our great fear is not that we might lose the friendship of women (after all, so much of our sense of our gender identity is bestowed on us by men in the absence of women) but that we will lose the friendship of other men.

This fear may appear in the form of crisis in relation to one other man in particular, which forces on us an awareness of what we are allowing to happen. For each of us is just one man away from selling out our anti-sexism. All it takes is one situation with another man — a situation that will be different for each of us — a particular man whose company and esteem and companionship we most want, and we will sell out our convictions for that connection; we won't speak our beliefs in order to bond.[23]

The choice is a hard one: 'affiliation and assimilation with men, just falling in with men on men's terms; or separation and estrangement, self-defined isolation'.[24] To compensate for this one might easily take up with

a woman of feminist credentials. They may be friends or lovers, heterosexual or homosexual, married or single, living together or apart it doesn't matter; what matters is their public alliance. She will provide him with credentials of his own; a plastic laminated wallet card that says 'I have been approved by a feminist woman' and it will have on it her good name.[25]

But taking up with such a woman leaves us no better off; we merely feel we have abandoned our brothers, sold out our origins and lost the right to see things from a male viewpoint, as all that is left is agreement with the woman on whose arm we are paraded. So other men put us on the spot, because we must decide and show where we stand.

Try the following. Men know what happens if a woman in the workplace brings up something that she finds sexist — a joke, an innuendo, a comment, a calendar, a memo, an overheard comment between two male colleagues. She will be told, 'We weren't serious'; 'That's not what we really meant'; 'It's not important'; 'It's not supposed to be taken that way'; or, worse

Other Men

still, 'You're overreacting' and 'You're paranoid/imagining it/touchy about it/frigid/humourless/joking, aren't you?' But try waiting till one of your male colleagues starts a story with one of the usual lines — 'Hey, have you heard the one about the blonde and the baboon/the window-cleaner and the wife/the gay guy with gonorrhoea?' — and saying loudly but firmly, 'That sounds rather an offensive start; why not try telling a genuinely funny story?' and see what happens. It won't be so much what happens at the time, the embarrassed 'Huh?', the bemused 'What are you on about?', the outright aggressive 'What's it to do with you?'. It's what happens later, when you are actively excluded from that circle, not just when they're telling the same kind of jokes in the corner of the office round the water-cooler/coffee urn/beer keg/bar, but at other times as well. See how you feel then. To confront other men with your views, as many feminist women do daily, puts a distance between you and them which creates considerable anxiety.

In the case of other men we must balance the books, emotionally speaking. This means being prepared to try to give some real form and expression to our deep and affective relationships with the straight men we know, as well as extending our sense of friendship to include gay men. This will lead to some animosity and hostility from women, as they are the gate-keepers and monitors of their partners' heterosexuality, and will wish to have it ever flowing towards them. But we must make this effort.

So much of our behaviour around men is based on a suppressed homoeroticism. Chester Eagle's *Play Together, Dark Blue Twenty* is an account of his years at Melbourne Grammar in the late forties and early fifties. Though it seems to be a narrative that endorses a heterosexual alignment in the school setting,

Junk Male

there are moments of disquiet. One of these is the morning parade to the showers:

> Heading for the showers in the mornings we have to walk the long aisle between the three dormitories of beds; four, if we're in the East. Some of us go towel over shoulder, displaying; it's said that F.T.'s brother, who left before we reached senior school, walked with a pair of footy boots dangling from his penis by their laces. Others move through, erections hardly softened; pricks are like reputations. It's a way of valuing ourselves, just as the masturbation which shows itself in the puffy skin at the collar of our mostly circumcised penises is a way of exploring the strange incarnation which has taken place inside our bodies. We're full of . . . the Holy Spirit, in chapel; in the dormitories, a grey-white glue that spurts at the insistence of our hands, or even, in the middle of the nights, our imaginations. We hate wet dreams just before we wake because they haven't dried out by the time we get up; everyone understands, but it's still embarrassing. Have we then nowhere to go? We've sexuality without partners, a force without an answer. SUNDER![26]

The word 'sunder' is the final word of the first line of the school song, which gives the book its title. The line in full is: 'None our ranks shall sunder.' At sporting occasions they end the lines by repeating the last word in a savage roar. 'SUNDER!' cutting across and emphatically ending a discussion of arousal in an all-male situation indicates the utter prohibition against any consideration of homoerotic bonding. There can be no recognition of the possibility of attachment between boys, for the expression of homosexual choice destroys in an instant the

Other Men

fragile and precarious adolescent heterosexuality that the boarders' masculinity has at its core. If they have 'sexuality without partners', then the 'answer' is not other boys. Men must 'sunder'; separate and keep apart from each other by fixing their sexual object choice on women.

Other men, therefore, are a challenge to us. The defensive homosocial sites of Australian male life see men interact with apparent intimacy, yet the same force that sees men seek out the company of men to validate their gender identity also sees them edge warily away from each other, as to get too close is to risk allegations of homosexuality. The full power of hegemonic masculinity can be seen in the way in which heterosexuality has become the definition of normality in Australia, and this means that the 'other men', gay men, ever present and unacknowledged, have been written out of the literary history of this country. The buried story of the strong thread of potentially homosexual affection that runs through Australian male interaction has been suppressed as too troubling and complicating to male heterosexist myths, despite the evident homoeroticism and rich sentimentality that men have towards men. The challenge, then, is to act upon that vein of strong fellow feeling, and try to translate it into some more relaxed and real social forms.

WORK

Why should I let the toad *work*
Squat on my life?
Can't I use my wit as a pitchfork
And drive the brute off?

Six days of the week it spoils
With its sickening poison
Just for paying a few bills!
That's out of proportion.

>> Philip Larkin, 'Toads'

He learned something of the trade [of plumbing] because he was quick at picking up things he liked to learn, on the principle that 'You can never tell what might come in handy one day' — years later he could expertly fix drains or 'wipe a joint', and his soldering was something to see — but the impression he gave at home was that all he was learning was how to get drunk with his workmates on Friday pay afternoons and various ways of driving Old Foley [the owner of the business] to the point of a nervous breakdown.

>> George Johnston, *My Brother Jack*

TO BE A MAN IS TO WORK

Men believe that work offers some form of self-actualisation; at some level and in some way, ourselves are brought out and given free play through work. What it offers in fact is no such scope, as it is merely another arena in which men play a role that is to do with a man 'being somebody because of his work and this gives him access to the world of men where his identity as someone is secure', just 'another battle-ground, where hierarchies are sought after, power is everything, and the return of satisfaction is often minimal'.[1] So while work offers much that is positive and empowering, it can also contain much that becomes destructive and embittering; a man's job 'separates him further from himself, as he is the first to admit. But as much as he acknowledges this, he also recognises that without his work he would be totally destroyed'.[2]

If home is dominated by the mother, then when a man leaves home for work he leaves it for a place dominated by the masculine 'organisational father . . . whether it is in a factory, a university, an office, a school . . .'[3] While initially this association offers power and status, in the long run it may represent yet another bad exchange. 'Once having opted to be with the "father" — in adulthood represented by the factory, the corporation, or whatever — men find it impossible to move, psychologically speaking',[4] and end up caught in a rigid, inflexible conservatism.

Junk Male

If work is male, then the son is introduced to the workplace by the father. For the son to see his father at work is a vicarious experience of power. Sidney Nolan felt this thrill at the proximity of power when he travelled with his father, an experienced tram driver in Melbourne at the turn of the century:

> Sidney was proud of the assured manner in which his father drove a tram, often taking long rides with him across town, feeling superior to the other passengers because he did not have to pay, as the conductor with a bell on his ticket punch passed him with a wink instead of collecting his fare.[5]

In this scene, the young Nolan is allowed into the masculine world of work. He sees his father's power, which rests on his competence and skill in handling the cable tram's controls, never an easy task, and the conductor with his wink makes him feel a subtle sense of superiority as he is within the world of work and men, unlike the other passengers.

To be a man is to work. Paid work is 'a major element in men's sense of who they are, including their sense of sexual identity'.[6] From observation of their fathers, sons see work 'personally experienced, as a life-long commitment and responsibility'.[7] This close linking of work and masculinity might explain the great vehemence which characterises all current discussions of workplace reform. For men, their very concept of self is structured around work as an activity. A man will talk of 'the "right to work", implying that work itself is necessary for his psychological well-being'.[8]

While men may initially come up with a rhetoric of value centred on the home, the family, the wife, loyalty to hearth and children, soon attention will shift elsewhere, and it will become

Work

apparent that much of a man's sense of self is created elsewhere. Work is a central arena to a man in which he establishes and maintains an identity.

> It is difficult for men to break with an instrumentality that has come to dominate so much of their life. It is as if men are often not available in relationships, their thoughts constantly drifting off. Real life and real work exist elsewhere, so that it can be hard for men to put their energies into relationships. Often we arrive at home too exhausted, drained and used up. Our best energies have been used up at work and we rarely hold ourselves back so that we have something to give when we get back.[9]

Mental habits acquired at work, such as the compartmentalisation of the day, the definition of tasks and delegation, often to a man's advantage, are difficult to leave behind, and frequently bleed over from the world of work into the world of home.

Subjectively, an unemployed person will experience a loss of meaning in his life; '"worklessness" involves a feeling of "worthlessness"; a sense of failure, which cannot be rationalised away'.[10] This might be because a man's ability to produce (as in the verb 'father', whether it be ideas, money or children) is central to his sense of a stable and achieved self. If his 'symbolic power (his wage or salary) is destroyed, a man's personality is undermined'.[11] For some, there even appears to be a connection between the life of work and life itself.

> You know, it amazes me, the amount of drivers I've known who have retired from driving and died very quickly

afterwards. Because I think, you know, that they have been keyed, or tuned rather, to a certain pitch. To a pitch where their bodies and minds were disciplined to total concentration. And then to suddenly have it all taken away. Nothing to concentrate on anyway, except pottering about around the garden, or letting the pigeons out, or something like that. I can give you cases at 'The Austin' [a British Leyland factory in the Midlands of England]. I've known four or five drivers who I've known to be physically perfect. And they've retired, and six months later we've been having a branch representative at the funeral.[12]

The purposeless 'pottering' implies that there was nothing of equal value to replace work once their life as a worker had ended.

For uncertain men, the workplace may allow an identification with a machine which improves their confidence. When Peter started work at a small engineering firm he was allowed to drive a

Ford Transcontinental ... at that time the most advanced truck of its kind on the road in Britain and Peter was like a child with a new toy at the wheel of his $500,000-worth of machinery ... The Transcontinental had a physical presence that matched its price. The bed of the trailer was a good five feet off the ground and eye-level for the driver was five feet higher than that ... The height, combined with the sense of mass and speed, seemed to invigorate Peter and fill him with the confidence he normally lacked.[13]

The most simple thing to be gained from work is the self-esteem that comes from the mastery of a skill.

Work

WORK AND ASSIMILATION

To join a workplace is more than merely to undertake work and be paid. It is to join a tight-knit group, which has a shared identity of masculine cultural values and views on how life ought to be lived. The ability of the individual to retain an independence of judgement in the face of the group's coercion to conform is doubtful. The poet Kenneth Slessor's father, a metallurgist, left his son an account of his early years in the infant mines of Tasmania. The senior Slessor was hampered by a culturally different background highlighted by a name not then anglicised, Schloesser. He remarked of his workmates that

> they were ignorant rule of thumb men, and great drunkards. In fact, when I joined the Mine Manager's Association and attended a few meetings, the remark was made, 'Funny sort of manager Slosher [sic] is — doesn't get drunk and knows no smutty stories'. I was not such a saint as that but had been through it all before. Certainly most of these managers made beasts of themselves — rather that is an insult to the beasts. [One of the managers said] his idea of luxury was 'To have a good dinner and plenty to drink and to sit afterwards with a plump tart on my knee and smoke a six penny cigar into her hair'.[14]

The form of the social interaction, drinking and smutty stories, seems to have remained the staple fare of male socialising in the workplace ever since.

Assimilation into the workplace by a man's workmates can be signalled by things as slight as the bestowing of a nickname. The attempt at a nickname in the case of Slessor's father seems to indicate that the others are ready to accept him, though the nickname depends on a punning mispronunciation of the surname, and indicates the expected nature of his involvement with the Association. In David Ireland's grim satire of industrial Australia, *The Unknown Industrial Prisoner*, the men are known by their nicknames alone; 'Sump-Sucker', 'Great White Father', 'Samurai' and 'Blue Hills' being some examples. Throughout the novel neither home, the rest of Australia nor the world has any existence or meaning, and we are invited to see only the men and their work as important.

For the boy joining the man's world of work, his 'membership was formally sealed through the "initiation ceremony" — practical joking, "debagging" (removal of trousers), and even forms of "tarring and feathering"'.[15] Just how these rituals are endured will determine how well the boy progresses into the workplace and how high he will stand in the estimation of his workmates as a worker and man. Sometimes practical jokes and debagging are combined:

> 'Does anyone not know the three-man lift?'
>
> 'I don't,' said Ambrose [the new apprentice]. Bubbles [the older worker] couldn't believe his luck. Soon they had one man sitting on the floor gripping Ambrose's ankles, another sitting behind him gripping his arms behind his back and Bubbles stood over them as if ready to lift the three men locked together. But instead of lifting, Bubbles bent down and searched until he found something belonging to Ambrose, a pretty little thing with a small, pink mouth and wide glowing cheeks. He held it up between finger and thumb, showed everyone, then got out the black boot polish he used to smarten up with when he went straight from work to the club and blacked this little thing all over.[16]

Work

Always the focus of the horseplay is the sexual, accompanied with profanity or obscenity.

> Pommy Bill, a small cockney sparrow, stood flushed and pleased . . . But just then a merry ex-Bomber Command pilot came up behind Pommy Bill, inserted a claw between his legs and grabbed joyfully and vigorously at his genital cluster.
>
> 'Gotcha!' he roared. Pommy Bill had his own private ascension.
>
> 'Jesus!' he screamed on his way down.
>
> 'Christ!' came the antiphonal from the faithful.
>
> 'The same yesterday, today, and forever!' added Bomber Command solemnly.
>
> 'Amen!'[17]

THE ROLE OF INITIATION AS A MEANS OF EXCLUSION

While the focus of the initiation is to create a 'male solidarity in the face of routinised drudgery and hard labour',[18] this does not mean that men care much for each other in actuality, as once again the competitiveness of the workplace activity keeps men separate and splintered among themselves. For a man's social 'acceptability is defined in terms of his dramatic self-presentation',[19] and therefore social status is not established merely by entry into the workplace; it must be maintained constantly in the face of ridicule and humiliation from other workmates.

A major assumption about the workplace is that it must be made free of sexual harassment by men of women in order to be a place of equality. However, there has been a very long tradition of harassment of male workers by other male workers, especially

Junk Male

in the skilled trades. In George Johnston's *My Brother Jack*, David Meredith encounters initiatory games in the commercial art studio in which he is an apprentice. There are two forms of harassment, directed against the same sexual targets as in Ireland's factory, one form being darts, the other the 'turps game'.

> Each artist had his own collection of home-made darts; little feathered blocks of wood pointed with used phonograph needles which would be aimed with considerable force at the backside of any artist who stooped too temptingly over his work. There were many times when I got home to find my underpants spattered with blood and my buttocks fiery with pain.[20]

The 'turps game' is even more painful:

> Our high stools had circular concave seats; the idea was that while the artist was engrossed a pool of raw turpentine would be spilled surreptitiously into this concavity; when the artist at last sat down to rest his aching arms and back, the turps would soak through his trousers to the infinite agony of his private parts.[21]

The effect of this ruse on one target was to send him 'clutching his balls[,] . . . roaring through the factory like a maddened bull'.

The sexual focus of these games is a clear indication of the role of the activity. The sexual immaturity and vulnerability of the target is being forcibly drawn home to him. Considering the number of darts the apprentice Meredith has suffered from, it is clear that this is his lot as the initiate. In a revealing phrase, Meredith comments 'one had to take it all in good part and try for revenge'. This is the comment of someone uncritically accepting the need for the activity and acquiescing in its role in the workplace. In that phrase the apprentice has accepted the buried ideology and begun to progress within it, as he realises that he must try for revenge. Perhaps in time he himself will lead in the 'turpsing' and dart-throwing a new apprentice.

Such traditions need to be challenged, as they are methods by which unwanted people can be actively excluded by those already in the workplace. It is as important for men as for women that they should thus be reformed or eliminated. In 1997 a nineteen-year-old apprentice, David McHugh, who was working at a cabinet factory in Williamstown, Melbourne, had the satisfaction of seeing the former director of the company where he had worked being fined $10 000, and the director's company fined an additional $50 000, for bastardisation which McHugh suffered while working at the factory. Some of the treatment that McHugh suffered was to be set alight, thrown into a bin full of broken glass, and bound and stapled to a board in the crucifix position. Asked why he initially accepted such behaviour, McHugh answered, 'I didn't know any better and they said they did worse things to others, so I just put up with it.'[22]

In imagining the defences put forward by those who bastardised McHugh, one can hear their lack of insight. 'It was just a joke that got out of hand'; 'He couldn't hack it'; 'He got upset'; 'He over-reacted'; 'What else can we do?'; 'But we've always done this'. In these words we hear the rejection of guilt at the practice, their confidence at their own rightness, and their failure to realise the true focus and effect of their attacks. Such practices have a distinct social cost; McHugh was off work for long periods because of his injuries, and spent three months as an in-patient of a Melbourne clinic as a result of the pronounced depression he underwent. This case, and other examples of practical jokes by older workers on apprentices involving fire that nearly killed the apprentices, is encouraging for the fact that the silence surrounding such 'pranks' has been lifted.

SEXUALITY AND GENDER IN THE WORKPLACE

The stand against the dominance of initiation practices or the relentless parading of sexuality — overtly heterosexual, though covertly homosexual — is to risk being seen as standing against the solidarity of men in the workplace and therefore to stand outside the limits of acceptable behaviour. Enormous pressure is brought to bear on such a man to make him stand in line, and this is another of those moments at which we see men policing men to achieve unanimity. Here is an account of one man's attempt to challenge the practice of putting up nude photos of women in the State Housing planning office where he worked:

> He was accused of being a pervert, it was implied he was homosexual — the term itself of course being used as a term of abuse — he was not fit to be a local Government Officer and his work was no good anyway. None of these accusations . . . was true, but another man did a character assassination of him in front of his supervisor, from whom he was expecting support. Far from being supported he was browbeaten. When this failed he was given a patronising homily on 'all working together as a happy family', etc. He then challenged his superior to make a statement that all

Work

naked pictures should be removed of both men and women; this was refused on the grounds that pictures of women are 'normal' and those of men are not. He was then threatened with dismissal.[23]

If it is that hard for a man to confront the sexism of the workplace, some understanding of how much pressure is placed on women who make equivalent challenges can be gained. At least the young male has in his sex one guarantee of advancement; all that is required is his good-humoured acquiescence in the rituals of bastardisation by older males that he sees going on around him. A woman has no such chance of acceptance: her sex places her forever outside acceptance.

Tania Wedge's perception of such a situation reflects an analysis of the same kind, but from a woman's viewpoint and from behind the glass wall of exclusion and rejection between herself and her male colleagues. Tania Wedge worked for five and a half years as one of the first women bus drivers with Transperth, the public transport company of Perth, Western Australia. She suffered constant harassment from the older male drivers at the depots, harassment that caused her and other women drivers much humiliation, anger and confusion. Though she left Transperth in the end because of a back injury, a significant factor in her decision was the thought of returning to the pressure of the harassment. 'It was a case of "if you can't handle it, get out",' she said. 'Every second word was an "f" word or worse.' In her view of the depot situation,

> The older men were the worst. They were set in their ways and couldn't adapt to change. I was in the depot for five and a half years and didn't even know some of their names. They

keep in their own little cliques and wanted nothing to do with
you. Even guys have had to leave because of interference in
their personal lives.[24]

Efforts by both men and women are needed to break the vicious
and malevolent resistance of such cliques of senior men in the
workplace.

That so much of male workplace horseplay is explicitly
sexual in its focus raises questions about the sexuality of the
workers themselves. Certainly, it seems to be an 'opportunity
for some to display latent homosexuality but certainly not to
come out'.[25] It may highlight the constant tension among all
male groups between the need to acknowledge homosexual
affection while at the same time performing a charade of
public heterosexuality. For displays of affection and actual
bonding between men are not part of the workplace: '[A]ny
sign of emotional dependence of one man on another is
instead an invitation to take the mickey. Such dependent
relationships are seen as more appropriate to a woman in
marriage.'[26]

A FRAGILE CAMARADERIE

This leads to the central contradiction of men's presentation of
themselves and their sexuality in the workplace. While men
display solidarity and comradeship there, this does not translate
into effective working group action, either informally in the
social settings of the office or pub, or in the more formal setting
of the union or a dispute between employees and employers.
The working man's 'stereotypical image of self was assertive,
independent, powerful and sexually insatiable'.[27] However, those

same workers could not escape the realisation that they 'worked the longest hours in the most insecure and tightly controlled jobs, enjoyed the worst canteen and car park facilities and the poorest holiday, pension and sickness provision ... [which] confirmed that they were the least valued and most easily disposable of employees'.[28] Therefore it might be said that the socially constructed role of the worker is to act as a carapace against the knowledge of powerlessness: '[W]ithout this defensive, cultural shield, a man would be too directly exposed to the humiliation of his position.'[29] Once again, we return to that common factor in men's presentation of self: a good deal of self-inflation in order to camouflage or gloss over the actual vulnerability of the self.

When the camaraderie of men in the workplace is actually put to the test, it is revealed to be no more than a fabrication, an illusion. This fragility has been revealed in more than one study of men in the workplace. Towards the end of one research period in a factory the decision to close the plant was announced, which would mean the loss of 153 jobs.

> Rather than reinforce the men's solidarity to fight (at the minimum) for improved redundancy payments, this decision merely exacerbated the fragmentation of the workforce. Against the advice of the trade union, the workers voted to accept the lump sum package without a fight.[30]

When faced with a similar erosion of their wages and conditions at the Puroil Factory, the workers in David Ireland's novel *The Unknown Industrial Prisoner* meekly accept the managerial recommendations. Only one voice is heard to comment on this craven collapse of the will to fight, so much at variance with the contempt expressed by the male workers of the refinery at other times for the 'bastards upstairs':

> An unidentified man fidgeting in the body of the hall half-rose to his feet and said half aloud, 'We're all pissweak.' Those near him heard him clearly enough, glanced mildly at him and puffed mildly on their cigarettes and pipes, as his bottom sank back where it belonged, but those farther away, eager to be diverted by any interruption, leaned their heads towards their neighbours, nudged and asked, 'Whadesay?' from the side of their mouths. 'We're all weak as piss', was the usual mild answer.[31]

RECONCILING REASON AND ANGER

The middle-class experience of work is qualitatively different from the working-class experience, but related in form. Whereas a working-class man is dominated by the process — the physicality — of work, the middle-class man's work is 'less of a physical experience performed in the company of others; more a lonely inner struggle to achieve'.[32] In addition the professionally aspiring must acquire a wholehearted identification with a sense of 'duty' or 'obligation', a moral justification absent from the work undertaken for a wage. This discipline is

> not the impersonal discipline of factory production, but self-discipline, an internalised desire to work. This desire is sustained by a man's faith in an authority greater than himself; an Empire, the Nation, or at a local level, the 'community', 'civic pride'. His ethical code, and the 'self-respect' which it confers, is what drives a man . . .[33]

Work

It is this internalised 'desire to work' in the service of others that drives me to work as hard as I do as a teacher. Nevertheless I am well aware that 'the values of "dedication" and "commitment", still supposedly attached to the teaching profession, are ... a source of exploitation'.[34] With these understandings and conflicts going through my mind every day at work, it is not surprising that I find my 'personality is the focus of an immediate contradiction between "authority" and "disobedience"'.[35]

The anger that builds up at work as a result of men's perceived powerlessness is a problem, for where can it go? What are its legitimate targets? Frequently the accumulation of strain and fatigue means that there is a need for release. Some men may manage their anger through alcohol, which gives an external sanction to explosions of temper. These men

> seem cool enough but at the end of the working day go off to the pub and then return to the office 'to speak their mind'. What they really want to do is fight out the difficulties they were unable to verbalise during the day when they had to try and keep their feelings under wraps.[36]

What might happen if that anger were channelled towards the work conditions that drove those men to such frustration?

Anger is not dealt with well by men in their relationship with work.

> 'Anger' appears as a 'threatening emotion', because it brings the possibility of challenging power. So [the angry worker] can be made to feel that because other people are putting up with a lot worse at work, he should, especially as a man

who can take the pressure, be 'reasonable' and put up with his lot.[37]

Thus the worker's feeling of anger is eroded and its authenticity is brought into question, as the worker is anxious not to lose his masculinity by allowing the suggestion that he can't 'take the pressure'.

This clash between anger and reasonableness is played out in industrial disputes, in which the workers are portrayed as acting out of anger, and therefore the first resort of management is to assume the voice of reason. In one clash between the members of the Metal and Engineering Workers' Union and Hamersley Iron at Mount Tom Price in Western Australia, for example, there were 'ugly clashes', and a spokesman for Hamersley Iron could say 'the company has been shocked by the depth of anger on the picket line'. However, it is the company's representative who is able to sound moderate and placatory by saying 'the scenes are ugly and unnecessary and it's time for reason to prevail'.[38]

Significantly, in the reporting of the incident there are references to long-term Japanese perceptions of the reliability of the Australian labour market, cuts by Brazil and Japan in their purchases of iron for the future, and the cost of the strike, but there is no attempt to redress the exact focus of the workers' anger. This is a working out in public of the private dialogue between reason and anger that occurs within all men dealing with injustice and frustration in the workplace. In the end the male worker is appealed to on account of things greater than himself — the national interest, the future — and he will give in when such huge interests are put against his own. So once again he is asked to be 'loyal to a shadow and obedient to the shadows of shadows',[39] and real reform of the workplace and his life are once again deferred.

RE-ASSESSING WORK'S CONSERVATIVE VALUE

Work does create tensions for men that are difficult to reconcile or regulate. While work may appear to promise much to the young male, eager for an expansion of his powers and horizon, the reality of the workplace is different. The first challenge to be overcome is the circle of friendship which unites the men in the workplace he is seeking to enter. He may have an adequate level of the required skill, but will he submit to the initiation games perpetrated on him by his fellow workers in the correct spirit, accepting his nickname as the union card of masculinity in the workplace, and by his silence acquiesce to the things that he sees going on around him? Or will he refuse to go along with the rituals, feeling degraded and humiliated by them, and be inevitably crushed by the pressure of standing against the sexist practices in the workplaces from which his mates' disdain will expel him?

Once entry into the workplace has been achieved, there is no real guarantee that his colleagues will support him. His place in the hierarchy will be constantly eroded by the men around him, and he cannot count on his mates for any real help; whether it is in personal terms or in the matter of working conditions, any solidarity he senses is illusory. At the first sign of threat it collapses into a desperate selfishness. As his working life progresses, he will be plagued by mounting rage and frustration as well as a conviction that he is being asked to work towards something to which he has little allegiance or about which he has no real understanding, such as 'increased productivity', 'workplace reform', 'overseas competitiveness' or 'reduced trade deficit'. A sense of pride and self-worth is replaced by a sense of having been conned. This experience of the life of work is little different for the middle-class professional, whose very values, so assiduously absorbed through slavish imitation and self-proselytising in youth, will be used to assault and undermine his sense of value for work done.

Changes in the workplace and in the culture of work will cause greater levels of stress to men than women. It is not just a matter of women's increased representation in the workplace, it is also to do with changing work practices and workplace-based reform and innovation. The conservatism of masculinity is once again being revealed by the way in which men cling to work practices and forms of behaviour set by informal precedent which allow them some token influence, even though those practices might have been unchanged since early last century.

Men also need to renegotiate the line between work and other areas of their lives. Too often work encroaches on the time we have spare for our families to be effective fathers and involved husbands. And so we are wrenched away from the personal, private, profitable time we might spend with ourselves and others. Though there has been reluctance by men in the workplace to join in the micro-economic reform of the late eighties and nineties, as the male working population finds its privileges and social influence eroded, one factor will force men to change their working values: the likely permanent shrinkage in the labour market. From the sixties and seventies, when unemployment stood between two and six per cent, it has now risen to a steady level of eight per cent, and may even hover nearer ten per cent till the end of the nineties. If work as an

Work

activity creating personal and monetary worth has been central to a man's life, then a new generation of men may have to learn how to reconstruct their lives so that other things in combination achieve that centrality.

ARTIST

I am hearing the killing inside of myself.

James Gleeson, written on the painting 'On the Destruction of the Face as an Authentic Phenomenon'

Break the mirror to see what I am.

Dusan Merak (surrealist), title of a painting

The role of writing

If a man is defined by his relentless pursuit of public acclaim and a public persona, art demands the opposite: many sequestered solitary hours. Australian society has a deep distrust of solitary activity; a man must guarantee his masculinity by public exposure and constant presence in the arenas of men. Separation from the places of men, the sites at which masculinity is created, is seen as critical by its aloofness — one of the greatest sins an Australian man may commit. Art also implies an unhealthy interest in introspection, distrusted by Australian men, who must be always outward and unintellectual.

To be an artist is first a matter of self-definition. Kenneth Slessor's brother recalls a revealing event about the young poet's creation of himself as a writer:

> At Chatswood Ken built himself a tree-house in a gum-tree, out of planks and boards and an old oar, which no-one else was allowed to enter. He would retire there at weekends to read, ignoring the other children. He also preferred to do his homework there. Robin's determination to explore the secrets of the tree-house led to some typical revelations of Kenneth's character.
>
> Then came the day when my sister gave me a leg up and I got to see what was in the tree-house room. There wasn't much. It was clean, there were no flowers in the vases, there was an old vase that he'd pinched from the house, there was a

Junk Male

desk, a few books scattered about, *Boys' Own*, *Chums' Annual*, *Coles Funny Picture Book* with its rainbow cover, *Magnets* and *Gems*, Hurree Ramset Ram Singh, Fysher T. Fyshe ... and so on.

There were in the room a writing pad and a bottle of ink, a pen and some nibs. I was very careful not to touch anything, or so I thought, not to move anything. I described it all in detail to my sister when I got down again. And when Ken came home he accused me of breaking and entering his tree-house which I stoutly denied. And I said ... 'How do you know that anyone has been in your tree-house?' His reply was, 'The angle of my pen on the desk had been altered, and I knew immediately that someone had been in.' That's pretty good for a 12-year-old detective.[1]

Well before Slessor had his first work published he was seeing himself as a writer, creating an appropriate separate space for himself in which he could write and read. The space is an orderly one in which great store is set by the exact position of the pen. Any writer will recognise the ingrained, fetishistic writing habits, which once established are rarely broken for a writing lifetime. Slessor's response to his brother's lie, a perfect riposte, seems borrowed from the acute observation of a Fysher T. Fyshe or a Ram Singh.

In the life of a male writer, writing may be another way in which he acquires control over his emotional, intellectual or remembered life. As Anthony Storr says in his essay on the role of writing in Kafka's life, 'for some people, writing, or some other form of imaginative activity, is a way of survival'.[2] In discussing Jack Kerouac's life, for example, his biographer Ann Charters comments:

Artist

> [W]hen his writing was going well, or when his emotional life was less disturbed, he could keep all the pieces [of his life] in a kind of balance with each other. When any part of the clumsy structure started to slip, the rest of him fell apart with it.[3]

Even if the male writer's life is falling apart around him, if he can write he can hold himself together, demonstrating the paradox that art often defies life by extracting harmony from personal confusion.

ART AS WORK

Part of the problem with the arts in Australia is that, still being a simple frontier culture in some ways, we prefer the indisputable to the uncertain. No-one can doubt that a mark is taken in a Grand Final, or a catch in a World Cup match; we can watch the action replay. The mark will lead to a winning goal, the catch to a won match. But what of the value of a painting? Or a novel? While there is discussion and a lack of exactitude about the value of the art object and the work that goes into it, neither the artist nor the work will be valued. For art is not seen as real work in a society which values the visible, the physical and the literal over the hidden, the intellectual and the metaphorical.

Barry Humphries received a letter from one fan in the form of an advertisement for his show with the words scrawled across it: 'Take that shit off your face and do some work you lazy bugger.'[4] Art is not perceived as work, and therefore a central means of self-definition as male has been removed from the male artist. There is a deep distrust of the activity of writing in

Australia because it cannot be compared with any other means of earning an income.

The *Yacker* books of interviews with Australian authors, edited by Candida Baker and published during the late 1980s, sought to ally writing to the working tradition in Australia. These books concentrate on the 'yacker', the 'work' of writing, with the attendant pun on 'yacker', as in 'talk'. Thus writers are people for whom 'talk' — using words — is 'work'. The books consist of profiles of various writers with a focus on their work habits: where they work, their daily patterns of writing, and a representative page of manuscript from each author. This presentation of writing is a plea for writing's seriousness as work.

To work is to guarantee one's masculinity; to engage in inappropriate work is to risk losing the respect of the men around you. George Lambert's father made it clear to the youthful would-be artist: '[H]e urged George to begin fulfilling his "masculine" responsibilities; he told him, that is to say, to get a job'.[5] Art was not a real job. Lambert, however, overcame this by applying principles of trade to his work. He worked assiduously at his art, and by the time he came to perform his famous commission as official war artist in the First World War, he had come to regard himself as a 'tradesman who had come out to [Palestine to] do a certain job of work',[6] in the words of one of his fellow officers. By emphasising the merely mechanical side of the activity, and denigrating inspiration and temperament, Lambert was making the kind of call for respectability that Australians could understand. It is not surprising, then, that he was well accepted as an artist on his return to Australia. The tendency of artists to either over- or undervalue their activity points to a profound ambivalence about the value of their work and their place in society.

Artist

Australia's uneasiness with art is the uncertainty of a frontier society when faced by something with no immediately apparent functional value, and the usual dichotomy of a society based on sexist divisions of labour and roles. In this, Australia shares much with America. The following description of life in a far-west town in late-nineteenth-century America could equally stand for Australia at the same time:

> The world of art and literature, or self-improvement and learning — except as it related to 'book' farming — was almost exclusively a female domain. A man's community activities, other than church and holiday celebrations, began and ended on Saturday nights when the stores stayed open till midnight and all the men gathered at [the] General Store (on the porch in the summer, and by the stove in the winter) to swap stories.[7]

There are many connections to be made between the persona and role of the artist in America and Australia.

For many Australians and Americans in the 1950s and later, art meant homosexuality. As the saying goes 'Bondi Boys Don't Paint'. Humphrey McQueen astutely observes that the art dealer Rudy Komon deliberately retained a 'vulgar veneer. As a man's man, he put at ease those executives who suspected that painter meant poofter'.[8] To be an artist was to be fatally mired in narcissism and effete in the popular imagination.

The male artist suffers a number of drawbacks in electing to become an artist. When he does so he must stand for feeling over intellect, and must stand or fall by the display of that feeling, whether it be in words or a visual medium. This goes against the essential male Australian taboo of silence on matters of feeling:

Junk Male

feeling is seen as a female preserve. The artist seeking to live by and with feeling, then, is seen as potentially effeminate. George Lambert, pressed by B. E. Minns of the *Bulletin* to choose between the manly life of the bush and the life of art, remembered the decision as

> the hour wherein I realised that I was not as other men. That before me stretched the long and weary road that is trodden by those who would attain greatness in the Arts — a veritable giving up of all that makes life bearable.[9]

There is no sense of optimistic challenge and the high calling of the artist; there is only a dulled recognition that art meant losing contact with so much that a man might enjoy as a man among men in shared 'real' work.

THE ARTIST AND THE MOTHER

Part of the problem for male writers is the origin of their abilities. To be a writer is to be willing to go into what are traditionally regarded as feminine preserves: the world of words and emotions. Artists from Henry Lawson to David Williamson have been identified as having skills that were recognisably those of their mother. Williamson's mother 'had a quick sardonic sense of humour and was adept at putting people down',[10] and when Williamson's wife met his parents for the first time in 1972 she 'remarked to him that it was obvious why he had become a playwright — it was growing up listening to that quick witty repartee, the acidic flavour of which'[11] is to be seen in so many of Williamson's scripts. The mother's example is clear, but this implies a role to be played by the son; by imitation he flatters and

Artist

gets attention. A photograph in Brian Kiernan's biography shows Williamson after having been awarded an honorary degree from Sydney University, and its caption reads: 'The Doctor of Letters amuses his mother at a celebratory lunch in Glebe after the conferring.' This seems to indicate that patterns of pleasing by verbal virtuosity acquired early in life take a long while to die.

The preceding are examples of the mother–son relationship as positive, but there can also be a negative side. Behind the stage persona of Barry Humphries, that master of staged sadism in the character of Dame Edna, is the intention to destroy the original. Humphries as a child dreamed of being a magician because that meant he could make people disappear. As Dame Edna, Humphries disappears, but he turns into a form that allows him to humiliate those who made his early life a particular hell. His whole act is to do with revenge. As he grew up with a desire to 'murder [his] parents', he decided to invent a persona that would allow him to 'murder them symbolically on stage'. But Edna 'is, among other things, a son's disturbing view of his mother', and the revenge Humphries takes on his hapless audiences is really focused on his mother, to repay her for her 'power to be at once the agent of joy and the means of eradication'.[12]

Another example of the way in which the alliance of the artist with the mother can work negatively appears in George Johnston's *My Brother Jack*, when David Meredith brings home his first means to being a writer, a heavy Remington manual typewriter. This provokes a violent outburst from Meredith's father: 'Get that infernal bloody contraption out of this house, this minute, you, and either come back without it or don't come back at all.'[13] At this moment David's father aligns him with his mother's family: '[H]e's become like the rest of that damned worthless, rotten, stuck-up family of yours...' This alignment is more than merely implying some congenital weakness, inherited through the mother's side, as David is seen by his father as following in another David's path: 'He's decided he'll follow in the footsteps of his wonderful bloody namesake... that brilliant writer... his clever Uncle Davey! That waster of a brother of yours who's drunk himself and his family into the poorhouse!' The link is with an alcoholic failure of a man, who would not fully perform the traditional role of breadwinner, but through the maternal side of the family.

CAMOUFLAGE: DANDY OR MACHO

As a reflection of their insecurity, artists in Australia seem to assume two compensatory roles for the sake of camouflage and protection within a society they perceive as hostile: the role of the dandy or that of the macho. The dandy seeks to escape into arcana and the past, and takes up satire, derision and vitriol, in the way that Barry Humphries has done. The macho writer takes up the challenge of making up for his writing or painting by strenuously engaging in the most ferociously masculine activities, especially drinking, womanising and tests of physical skill, as did George Lambert.

At various stages in their careers artists may use either method of camouflage. George Lambert set about developing an appropriately dandified public persona, and on his return to Sydney he would 'play the role of artist for all he was worth — striding through the city in billowing coats, stick in hand, and appearing at concerts and fashionable parties in immaculate evening dress'.[14] He developed this role to the point where it

Artist

obscured his real self in his self-portraits. In the self-portrait of 1921, for example, we see a

> work of extraordinary self-admiration. Dressed in a velvet robe, his now almost completely bald head bare, George poses against a black background with one hand on his hips and the other dramatically raised with its fingers spread. On a level with his groin, and pointing in a spray towards him, is a bunch of gladioli. It is a preposterously theatrical image of the artist as potent creator.[15]

It is not so unusual that a self-portrait by a male artist should be not about self-revelation, but rather elaborate self-deception and evasion.

That was how Lambert acted in Sydney, but when he was with the Australian Army in Palestine it was a different matter. There a fellow officer described him as

> a shaggy fellow with a jutting yellow beard and ultra-virile affectations ... An artist among soldiers (even an artist in uniform) is an unusual sight, but Lambert's manly bluster carries him along quite easily.[16]

Both were hard roles to live up to, and fatiguing facades to maintain.

BECOMING — AND STAYING — AN INSIDER

Artistic circles operate in the same way as other male groupings: a member of the group puts forward an invitation to someone outside the group to enter, or they in turn put forward the

Junk Male

outsider to the senior member of the group. A simple example of how an aspiring artist might be invited to join a group is given by Alister Kershaw in his account of Melbourne's bohemian circles in the decade from 1937 to 1947. In the opening pages he discusses Gino Nibbi and his Leonardo's Bookshop, a very potent arts site in the thirties, as it gave those who visited it 'the opportunity to buy, or simply look at, reproductions of quality and books and magazines dealing with art'[17] that were otherwise unavailable, so not only bibliophiles but artists congregated there.

> We venerated Gino. He was the boss. None of us really knew why. We didn't give a damn what anyone else thought of us but we candidly hankered after Gino's good opinion. However much or however well you wrote or painted or sculpted or composed, unless you had Gino's okay you didn't qualify as any sort of artist, not even in your own eyes. Acceptance by Gino wasn't signified by so much as a pat on the back, but somehow the news got around. From then on, you were taken seriously.[18]

Kershaw then goes on to describe as 'initiates' Albert Tucker, George Bell and Adrian Lawlor. It is significant that he does not name any women as initiates, even though the book does open with a description of Alannah Coleman, whom he defines as 'a bewitching young artist'. However, it does seem that 'seriousness' is reserved for the male initiates, and that in the end Alannah is merely 'an exceptionally attractive young woman'.

This is an example of a successful assimilation, but it is worth looking at how a woman saw such an event. In the early fifties, when poet Kenneth Slessor was in his early twenties, pubs

Artist

were still masculine precincts. The rich detail and smoke-blurred edges of the stories told from within the circle of Slessor's male journalist friends are starkly contrasted with Sylvia Lawson's memory of being introduced 'to the great man who seemed totally uninterested in conversation with your female journos, even when they'd published verse. I have a dim memory of feeling a bit peeved'.[19] Even though she had been introduced by a male member of Slessor's circle, Alec Sheppard, she was ruthlessly cut out; the process of initiation had been correctly undertaken, in that the novitiate had been proposed by a member of the group at the site, but membership was rejected out of hand because of gender. The gender lines for the ensuing twenty years of the visual and verbal arts in Australia were set, and these simple examples serve as the paradigms of how the essentially male groupings of that period and subsequent decades functioned.

In the assimilation of men into a group, dress is significant. While there is a tendency to regard dress as a means to recognition only when it is a uniform, there can be unofficial uniforms, codes of dress that proclaim a person's allegiance to others in the same group. Therefore

> any young man walking down Melbourne's Collins St [in the early 1930s] wearing a George V beard, for example, was unquestionably a [Max] Meldrum student, and it was said that one could tell how long he had been so by its length.[20]

For an individual who wished to become an artist, dressing correctly was at once a signal to those on the inside of the art world of the wearer's intention to join, or of their membership, and a flaunting of lifestyle to those outside the group.

Junk Male

Sidney Nolan made an attempt to gain some sponsorship for his intention to become a painter in 1940. Though the young Nolan had little or nothing to show that would prove his competence, he nevertheless went out to see various powerful people in the Melbourne art world. For this he knew he would have to dress appropriately.

> Nolan had always been a neat dresser, a habit acquired from his mother. Artists were not expected to look either neat or prosperous and Nolan knew it was essential to dress down for the encounters of the day ahead, putting on a pair of paint-spattered trousers, an old brown sweater with frayed sleeves and a pair of leather sandals, none of them part of his normal street wear.[21]

In many accounts of art and artists in Australia it seems that to look like an artist was more important than to create works of art. It didn't matter what you had actually achieved just as long as you looked the part.

A problem that reveals itself about male groups in the arts world is how, once an outsider has become an insider, a full member of the group, criticism becomes problematic. The network of association and acquaintance that goes with membership makes truly independent judgement impossible. In the thirties older artists were frequently granted positions on boards of trustees of galleries; this was certainly the case at the National Gallery of Victoria. When these artists, who had already received long-standing patronage from the gallery in terms of pictures bought, were co-opted onto the Board, their powers of critical separation from their recent benefactors were fatally flawed.[22] Membership of a male

Artist

grouping is predicated on the assumption that criticism will be suspended.

Inside the male groups, the interaction between males resembles the conversation that we hear among males in other settings: it is intensely competitive, designed to simultaneously destroy others' credibility while enhancing the speaker's, and to do with the ongoing struggle for ascendancy within the group. One setting for such conversation is the dinner table. The Sydney literary dinner table takes the lead from what Frank Moorhouse, the noted short-story writer, has called 'inventive verbal play',[23] in which a male speaker's ability is judged by how far he has exceeded the previous speaker in wit and devastation.

This is how David Williamson describes dinner-table conversation in Sydney:

> There's not much debate about politics and feminism. It's what you'd read, films you'd seen, and more esoteric matters, the better so you could decimate the other poor bastard's backwardness. It was supposed to be done in a charming, witty, inventive way. But the performances often didn't live up to the expectation, and many Sydney dinner dates were punctuated by huge silences as people tried to think of desperately witty things to say that would crush the last speaker.[24]

Williamson has changed his social patterns when it comes to going out for dinner; he has 'stopped accepting invitations to dinner parties in Melbourne, except those held by close friends'[25] because as Williamson has observed, such parties 'could get exceedingly unpleasant because people are more direct and brutal about questioning your life motives and more inclined to level charges that you are bourgeois and middle-class and frivolous and prostituting your art'[26] in Melbourne than Sydney.

ROLES DEFINED BY GENDER

The way in which artistic circles operate on patterns of behaviour that are distinctly male can be seen from the status and position that women have occupied in the arts in Australia since the turn of the century. Historically it is interesting to note that, according to one male art historian, the 'overwhelming majority of students [at the Melbourne National Gallery school in 1890] were either young girls waiting for their debutante ball or middle aged women concerned as much with permanent waves as with art',[27] yet by the 1940s, when there were the first serious and organised debates on the arts and their place in Australian society, such debates were dominated by men.

The pattern had changed by the forties to one of men producing and women consuming the arts, and that has since remained the case. A 1992 study of participation rates in cultural activities by the Australian Bureau of Statistics revealed that women have a higher participation rate than men in almost all cultural activities, including visits to art galleries, museums, libraries, music concerts, dance performances, and theatre. According to this survey, libraries were the most popular cultural venue, with 4.4 million visits made, while galleries were third most popular with 2.9 million visitors. But no matter what the venue, women had higher participation levels than men for all activities and across all age groups, with only a few minor exceptions. It still seems that 'art's just not the norm for blokes'.[28]

One setting in which the constant friction between men and women who aspire to be regarded as artists can clearly be

Artist

seen is the domestic site. In one account of such a site, a significant one in the production of much Australian art in the forties, nuclear physics is the metaphor used by a commentator to define the forces of attraction that keep the various satellites in their respective orderly orbits:

> The nucleus [at 'Heide', in Melbourne's Heidelberg] consisted of the four partners of the publishing firm; John Reed, Sunday Reed, Harris and, from 1944, Sidney Nolan. An outer ring included Albert Tucker, his wife Joy Hester, John Perceval and a host of satellites who came and went.[29]

Despite their centrality to many of the arts events and personalities of the late thirties and forties, 'Sunday Reed's thoughts were not published [and] Joy Hester's paintings and drawings were exhibited only rarely'.[30] While women occupy an important role in providing the domestic support and the essential routine necessary for some kind of social interaction in addition to the production of art, their role as possible commentators, or even artists, in their own right, is not recognised. They cannot aspire to centrality or 'seriousness' in the way that male artists do.

The social assumptions hinted at in public tended to be seen even more clearly in private practice. Nolan himself, when he was living at Ocean Grove before leaving his wife to go to Heide,

> went about his painting with a single-minded purpose that tended to ignore the fact that Elizabeth was a good artist as well, attempting to develop her own style. He appropriated the sunny end of the room they used as a joint studio and this domination led to growing strains and disagreements.[31]

Junk Male

In their private as well as public lives women were shouldered aside by the men.

The simple question of who does the cooking will tell more about the power structure and the views of those around the table than any account of the subjects discussed. For example, when Sidney Nolan arrived at Heide for the first time in 1938, he was 'greeted at the door by Sunday, who then disappeared into the kitchen to prepare their meal'. As Nolan and John Reed waited for the meal the serious talk began over a glass of whisky: 'Why do you think D. H. Lawrence had such an interest in sex?' was Reed's first comment. When the meal began Nolan noted a difference between Sunday's conversation and that of the men: '[Keith] Murdoch, [Basil] Burdett, [George] Bell and Reed had engaged him in straightforward conversations, masculine and direct, whereas Sunday's talk was intensely feminine, complicated and strangely disturbing.' This points to there being a qualitative difference between the men's and women's conversation in the same setting. In Nolan's biographer's account Heide is seen as an idyll apart from one thing: the 'hidden side to this apparently ideal marriage ... centred on Sunday's inability to bear children and the subsequent drift into casual relationships that developed within their circle'.[32] In the otherwise harmonious all-male circle, it is the woman who is the interloper, causing the final schism.

The arts setting is different from other male groupings in that there may be women present, but the nature of the networking going on between the men ultimately means that the women are marginalised and pushed to the edge of the circles, to become footnotes in the lives of male artists or writers. Even when women are present, men's networking can function effortlessly around them, still weaving patterns of men's power

Artist

even in a mixed environment. Looking at the photographs in Kiernan's biography of Williamson, it is worth noting that the majority are by Kristin Williamson, his wife. This gives her an interesting place; she is of but not with those people portrayed, documenting rather than really present. She appears by disappearing.

Two photographs in Kiernan's biography of Williamson are of special interest. One is of the Stenhouse Circle in the clubrooms of the Riverview Hotel, Sydney, 1989, and the other is of the dinner table at Geirstein, Williamson's Sydney house. Williamson has been photographed, chin ruminatively on hand, in front of that same dinner table, empty for a feature article on him for a national newspaper.[33] In each of the photographs there is a clear balance of the diners; women equal men in numbers, and all seem animated and involved in the speech or conversation. Yet in accounts of such dinners it is mainly the male guests whose presence is noted, and if significant discussions are recounted, they have occurred between the men. In recounting the genesis of the play *Money and Friends*, for example, it is only noted that Williamson was listening to the conversation at the house of comedian Campbell McComas, rather than who was actually making the observations about 'middle-class people used to financial security finding themselves in the lurch'.[34] So it seems that women are present, but their presence and contribution to debate are overlooked and ignored in subsequent accounts of such occasions.

The arts, then, also show signs of patterns similar to other areas in the way masculinity is created by male artists amongst themselves and how men can dominate gatherings of both sexes in such a way as to make their own concerns central, and to achieve status as 'serious' artists. Women, on the other hand, are shouldered aside, their art is trivialised and their contribution to the arts scene are belittled as being by pliant handmaidens to male genius. An interesting element in the history of the arts in Australia, especially in painting, is that, although women dominated the creation of art at the turn of the century, by the end of the Second World War they had been displaced by men, a process mirrored in America in the same period. This points to the ability of men to employ masculine behaviours in the infiltration of a new social area for the purposes of colonisation and domination of that area to their own material and social advantage. Art at the turn of the century was safely sentimental and feminine; by 1950 it had become aggressive, competitive and abstract, in other words — masculine.

In whatever setting women appear, the domestic setting of the dinner table, or the house as a unit of artistic production, or the state or private galleries, they cannot break into men's dialogue and present their own credentials to be regarded as equals, because of the dominance of masculine styles of behaviour.

TENSION IN THE ROLE OF ARTIST

As with many other public roles assumed by men, the identity 'artist' does not guarantee a stable persona; the writer is successful only till the next dinner party at which he displays his wit, the painter 'important' only till his next exhibition, both depending on a milieu that is supportive of their needs and structured around sustaining their worth. In a deeper sense, to become an artist in Australia is to be condemned to play out a life of self-inflation in constant conflict with an apathetic society in which family psychology is no help. To be an artist is to be

Artist

male, but not quite the right kind of male. This is perhaps clearest in the vigorous Australian art debates during the war years in which artists played out dreams of epic romantic grandeur. The following words describe the plight of American artists at that time, but they could be equally well applied to the Australian situation:

> [S]o many fathers considered it a crime against nature to be unmanly or 'unproductive', and so many mothers ... confirmed their aspirations by instilling in their sons delicate sensibilities and a respect for 'culture'. Given their upbringing, it was inevitable that male artists in the art world of the thirties, forties and fifties would be condemned to a constant struggle to appease their insecurities, to reconcile their fathers' injunctions with their mothers' aspirations; that they would all but exclude female artists from their company; that they would pass women around like bottles of whisky; that they would feel compelled to walk the barroom gauntlet, snarling insults, hurling profanities, and picking fights in a running parody of masculinity.[35]

Once again achievement and calm do not go hand-in-hand for men; the burden of proof is eternal, and must go on.

Art as an activity sets up contradictions within the artist's individual psychology. How can a man dedicate himself to a life based on qualities stereotypically feminine and at the same time expect what he does to be regarded seriously by other men as work? Faced by a frontier culture that lauds physical competence, taught by other men or the father to value the action over the word, how can an artist see as stable a role based on private, intellectual or emotional effort that employs the mother's skills? The resultant behaviour of the individual male is a measure of the strain felt in the role of artist, and is an attempt to deal with ambivalent status through postures. The over-dressed dandy and the macho, pub-frequenting artist are alike in that each is attempting to create a consistent masculine role — a public position from which the artist can operate — as well as camouflage and evasion of contact in order to establish private space for the life of the mind.

MURDER

I've always been afraid that ... control, control, there's that feeling that if you're pushed too far ... some little thing ... and you hit that button ... anger and fear and hate ... they're so close, mate ... survival, all you think of, up to a certain point ... then, beyond that point ... that state of mind ... you think of dying ... and you discover that dying's fucking *nothing*.

James McQueen, *Hook's Mountain*

I just know that I done it ... I get most of it back from dreams ... you gotta block things out ... you got to ... If you can't do it you won't survive.

John Travers, convicted for the murder of Anita Cobby

Uncontrollable urge or premeditated act?

The events of Port Arthur have again raised the question of men's readiness to use violence. Our horror and incomprehension of such actions are best illustrated by the hasty headlines talking of lost innocence, or making spurious comparisons with Port Arthur's history, as reporters grappled with the enormity of the situation. Suddenly everyone had become an expert in outrage and had ready for the cameras or the microphones their condemnation of the killer, followed by a simple explanation based on a single cause. Murderers have ready-made explanations available in journalistic accounts: '[T]he killer who tells us "I don't know what came over me", or "I really loved her" or "I was cleaning up the streets" is using a formula, a generic convention which he learned in society.'[1] These stock answers give little insight. Meanwhile, newspapers must have stories and headlines, and a simple answer is at least an immediate comfort, though it defers till later a fuller analysis of all the complexities.

In seeking to answer the question what such murderers have in common, it might be worthwhile to ask instead 'what makes a man violent? That which makes him a man. What do the child abuser, sadist, sexual murderer, serial killer have in common? Masculinity.'[2] In scape-goating murderers such as Martin Bryant with words like 'monster', 'fiend', 'demon' or 'maniac' next to a photograph retouched to show a suitably crazed expression, we lose sight of the fact that it is men who kill, and their training to be men which encourages them in their mistaken belief that they have the right to do so. Certain experiences of men in becoming or failing to become male mean that a man will see it as possible that he should kill others in order to prove his status as a man. If violence is dominated by men, and the 'linking thread between violent offenders is that they are male, then it is to masculinity itself that we must look for the answer to its origins and for any hope of its remedy'.[3]

Men's claims of uncontrollable urges that cause them to be violent — 'I just saw red', or 'I don't know what came over me' — belie the fact that violence is almost invariably contemplated or even planned before being carried out. It might appear that the multiple rapist, for example, is acting in an unpremeditated and spontaneous way, but the crimes seem to contradict such an interpretation. Raymond Edmunds, better known as 'Mr Stinky', used virtually the same forty words in the opening phases of each of his attacks.[4] While some of these were predictably designed to reassure and calm his victim, such as 'keep quiet' and 'don't scream', there were other revealing phrases such as 'I just want someone to love me', or 'I want to make love to you'. These, when combined with the circumstances of the crimes — a woman alone with small children, sometimes even in the same room, whom he had watched, sometimes for months — indicate that there was a clear plan in his mind, and that he was actually trying to create a specific scenario.

The rise of the serial offender has alerted society to the way in which individuals act out preconceived roles in their behaviour. The serial killer's 'signature', or recognisable combination of elements at a crime site, is repeated, which indicates an obsessive return to some original scene that has persisted in the killer's mind. Thus John Glover, the 'Granny

Murder

Killer' of Sydney's harbour-side suburb of Mosman and one of the few true serial killers in Australian criminal history, even in his first attacks on Winefreda Ashton in May 1989 had a sufficiently clear image in his mind of what he wanted to do that he left his signature: the walking stick laid parallel to the body, the shoes taken off and placed pointing towards the feet about a yard away from them, and the dress pulled up over the buttocks. As one of his biographers has commented, 'it was as if he had rehearsed the sequence over and over in his head',[5] and one detective had the impression that in looking at the crime site he 'was looking at the murderer's most intimate fantasy'.[6]

The plans of such men were formed during their otherwise normal lives, and were only revealed in pursuit of their particular scenario. To separate the man in crime from the man at other times is to separate him from society and thus ignore that he had been functioning as a competent member of society until detected. So with murderers and rapists the question 'is surely not whether these men were all insane; it is why so many men's madness takes this specific form'.[7] We are not looking at crimes that are motiveless; and for an explanation of these crimes we must look to the masculinity of the men who committed them.

A SHORT CUT TO SEIZING LOST POWER

Whether we are looking at mass murder, the murder of women by men, or men murdering men, central to each of these situations is the masculinity of the murderer and how it allows or encourages lethal violence. The origins of the attitude of the murderer towards himself, his victim, and society in general that suggest to him that murder is a possible resolution of personal crisis are to be found in his masculinity.

Junk Male

The mass murderers we have endured in Australia have been comparatively young: Frank Vitkovic, who shot eight people at the Telecom Office in Queen Street in Melbourne in 1987, was twenty-two; Julian Knight, who shot seven people in Hoddle Street also in 1987, was nineteen at the time of the killings. American examples show that the mass murderer is usually between eighteen and thirty-five, and this put Martin Bryant near the upper age limit. The question of what made them capable of such actions leads us to look at their lives. In a simple way, the origins of the process that saw them become intent on homicide can be traced to the same period in their lives: adolescence. John Travers' mother — though he was merely a single murderer, having cut the throat of Anita Cobby — put it clearly when she said in bewilderment that he 'was such a good baby, I can't understand how he grew up into such a little monster'.[8] Frank Vitkovic put it more poignantly in his final letter to his mother, finished hours before he began killing: 'Remember me when you carried me on your shoulders to kindergarten. Remember me when I was a bright boy of twelve who was so gentle and kind.'[9]

It is interesting that Vitkovic picks the age of twelve, before the teenage years when the attempts to achieve a secure masculinity begin. Most men will have achieved a relatively secure gender identity by twenty-five years of age — finished school, begun a trade qualification or entered university, perhaps begun to work, acquired a car, discovered a dependable peer group, a satisfying interest or hobby, involved in relationships of varying and deepening maturity with women. For others the years between fifteen and twenty-five will seem harder to negotiate without some major damage to the self-image and a perception that 'the world', 'the system', 'things' or, least

Murder

accurately, 'women' are to blame for a lingering sense of failure and lack of adequate recognition.

Mass murderers are frequently unable to tolerate frustration. Rejection can lead to cyclonic outbursts of temper. Over a varying length of time, sometimes as short as a week, perhaps as long as six months or more, the potentially violent man has been enduring a series of checks to his passage to manhood. These may range from failure in an exam or profession to rejection by a woman. In such cases the timetable of progress into masculinity has been delayed, and a 'short cut'[10] is taken. Mass murder is the failed male taking his revenge on a world which he sees as not recognising him sufficiently.

Both Vitkovic and Knight were frustrated in their career plans. While Vitkovic had done well enough at school, at university he did not perform as well, and after a bizarrely inappropriate answer in an end-of-year exam he gave up his university studies in Law. While being an industrious student had been sufficient at a secondary level, it was not adequate at tertiary level, and perhaps he felt keenly the weight of expectation on him to succeed. Knight, on the other hand, had suffered a more profound frustration in his chosen career path. His father had been a major in the army, and from an early age Julian Knight had been a keen cadet with an interest in military history and directed towards Duntroon. Once he had achieved that goal, however, the dream began to unravel as he had to confront the challenge of turning a long-held ambition into reality. Against a background of implied bastardisation and a confrontation with a sergeant-major in which Knight drew a knife, Knight withdrew when it became clear that he would not make the grade.

Both Vitkovic and Knight had difficulty in forming close links with the opposite sex. Vitkovic called his diary Sally because he had 'always wanted a girlfriend called Sally'. There is little evidence in the diary's pages that he formed any particularly deep or lasting relationship with a woman. Knight's links with women were more problematic. Certainly in the weeks and even the day preceding his rampage he had been involved with a girl his own age, and formed an obsessive relationship with an older woman, though his attentions indicated desire on his part rather than reciprocation on hers. It is significant that on Knight's return to Melbourne, after his unsuccessful attempt to become a soldier, a former girlfriend did not want to see him, and he was specifically excluded from a party that she held. At the Royal Hotel in Clifton Hill on the night of the shootings he tried to gain the attention of the older woman and the barmaids, unsuccessfully in each case. Just before he left the pub he punched a window in a state of rage. It is clear that women become the targets for male frustration, as the first person Knight shot was a woman. While Vitkovic also first shot a woman, that was because his first target, a male friend, had eluded his opening shot. It is worth noting that Wade Frankum, responsible for the Strathfield killings in which seven people were killed, also first killed a woman, stabbing a fifteen-year-old girl who was sitting behind him in the Coffee Pot Cafe in the Strathfield Plaza shopping centre in Sydney, and whose conversation he had probably been overhearing for the preceding hour or so.

Alcohol was a factor in Knight's actions. According to Knight's recollection and those of the patrons of the Royal Hotel, he had consumed between five and fifteen pots of beer while there. At half past eleven his blood alcohol reading was 0.088, which means that at half past eight, during the shootings, it would have been 0.1.

Murder

After the incidents, professionally qualified people made judgements about the sanity of each of the perpetrators. While Knight was judged fit to plead, he suffered an emotional breakdown in prison. The killings did not stave off the collapse of his own character in the short term, as murder may in some cases. While still alive Vitkovic was judged a borderline psychotic after having written the bizarre exam answer already mentioned, and after his death as a 'florid psychotic' by forensic psychiatrist Allen Bartholomew. While less material exists as to Vitkovic's state of mind it is at least clear that he felt the deep-seated animosity towards women, especially feminists and lesbians, typical of many serial and mass murderers. In his diaries he also shows the distance from the self that allows others to be regarded as less than human, and the self as being something to toss away. In this he saw his last actions as ones that would restore his devalued self, and make the rest of the world recognise his power. This is indicated in a diary passage in which he tips from first into third person, presenting himself in the way that Ted Bundy did in recounting his crimes, except that Vitkovic is looking forward to his crimes, whereas Bundy was looking back on his:

> I was the one who took it all. And the years go by and he continues to take it all. His resentment and hostility however are growing all the time. He feels so small, they made him feel so small, so useless, so small. He must redress the balance. He must restore himself to a higher position. He must become a bigger man than the enemy think they are if he is to conquer.

The causes of Vitkovic's state of mind were physically sited in his own body. A keen tennis player, an injury brought about by playing too much meant that he had to give up tennis, a sport in which he did well and on which much of his self-esteem was based. His doubles partner remembers his temper as Vitkovic tried to achieve 'errorless tennis', which reflected his perfectionism. A forensic psychiatrist said of Vitkovic that the injury would have been a 'threat to this man's physical and psychological integrity', as he invested so much in the game. His diaries contain records of scores of games in which he played, as well as other games.

ODD MAN OUT — OR PART OF THE WORLD?

Vitkovic also had a sense of being the 'odd man out', a recurring phrase in his diaries that has a clear meaning for him. It refers to the experience of undressing with his peers at the age of eight, and being discovered to have an unusual penis.

> Some boys looked at my penis in the change room. Look at Frank's his is different. It hurt my feelings a lot. It was a turning point in my childhood. Up till then I felt normal but after that I felt like the odd man out. Even in the toilet line they looked at my penis as if to say what the hell is that.

While a friend, David Bilusic, said 'it never seemed to bother him at the time' that he was called 'Vik the Dick', or 'Vik the Prick',[11] it is clear that Vitkovic was deeply upset by such comments, and a deep-seated rage towards his body increased as his weight ballooned during his inactivity from the tennis injury.

When Vitkovic talked of the past it was as if it were actually engraved on the body which he subsequently destroyed, as he talked of how the 'past is with you. Like the skin on your body

Murder

or the hair on your head, it is a part of you'. Thus he could escape the pain of his past by escaping his body.

Reading Vitkovic's diaries is a wrenching experience. One reads them like a novel in which the ending is known, but that does not stop one from grasping at the moments when he veers towards the positive, socially linked life that he needed for him to stop short of carrying out his increasingly violent intentions. At the one extreme he shows that he has absorbed the crude lessons of masculinity heard from a coach's lips and is able to string them together into a philosophy of cobbled cliches:

> Cop it sweet and battle on with all you've got left. That's the best philosophy. If you don't pour your heart into anything you can't possibly succeed. Give 100% and you can make it.

At other times a clearer voice is heard, one in which there is a sense of authentic emotion and a vivid character leaps off the page:

> The weather was really bad today. A lot of rain. I got really wet. It's a nice feeling. Walking in the rain with a rain jacket over your head, a bag over your shoulders and alone. Independent, a feeling of power grew over me as the wind pushed back my hair. I wasn't scared any more. I felt all conquering. I felt strong. I could sense that people in cars feared me. I looked mysterious, rain jacket pulled over my head you couldn't see much of my face. I like walking around like that. I like being the mystery man. Sometimes I am a mystery even to myself and they are the worst mysteries believe me. This rain just keeps falling and falling but I don't

mind. I've always loved the rain, the wind and the night. They make me feel small, just part of a huge world. All over the world people are living their lives. I'm just trying to get through mine.

In this extract there is a sense that the 'mysteries', even the mystery of self, are not unbearable, and that there is some stability in the self. The fear he imagines causing the passing motorists is merely the sense of the difference between the actual and augmented self that constitutes masculinity, but it is not a difference that will lead to violence in this case because with his rain jacket pulled over his head he becomes anonymous and absorbed into the world. And rather than a sense of distance and being the 'odd man out' there is some sense of being 'part of a huge world' which Freud described as 'a feeling of an indissoluble bond, of being one with the external world as a whole'.[12] Unfortunately moments of such calm connectedness are all too rare in Vitkovic's diaries.

AMBIVALENT RELATIONSHIP WITH POWER

Vitkovic's mental state at the time of his killings was one of florid psychosis and a general hatred for the world and women in particular; Knight's was significantly different but also revealing of the way in which the killer seeks to restore his self-esteem and achieve the respect of others. Knight was fixed on a military career from an early age, in emulation of an absent father, as his parents separated when he was quite young.[13] Absent or ineffective fathers are part of the overall picture. John Glover's father left his mother, and she had a succession of de facto relationships; John Travers' father left home because of the

Murder

violent arguments he and Travers had; and Raymond Edmunds, 'Mr Stinky', was an adopted child. An effective father figure who is emotionally present for the son seems a potentially strong stabilising figure. Knight's ambition was frustrated when he failed to fit in at Duntroon. He had always had a 'deeply held personal portrait of self as a soldier', as the clinical psychologist Kenneth Byrne said at Knight's trial, and this self-image remained despite his failure to achieve it in reality. Knight used this self-portrait to 'make himself feel better, to feel stronger, more competent and more masculine'.

However, it would seem that in trying to become a soldier he was attracted by the power held out by the role, but unwilling to submit to the authority necessary to achieve that power. This is a common fault in Australian men, who have an ambivalent relationship with power. They are all too ready to aspire to power, but when faced with a just authority their submission is not forthcoming. This contradiction means that relationships with authority figures such as police and teachers are likely to be stormy. John Travers, for example, the murderer of Anita Cobby, engaged in confrontations with his father and teachers, and was expelled from a school for exposing his penis to a teacher.[14] Yet he was unable to deal with those who did not accept his authority in turn when he expected them to do so; on one occasion he inserted his thumb in the anus of a younger brother because he would not do his bidding.[15] Travers and Knight wanted power without any of the rites of submission that precede power being bestowed.

Knight did not fit in at Duntroon. He was unwilling or unready to take his necessary place at the bottom of the hierarchical, clannish world of the army. One acquaintance said of him:

> [H]e just didn't have that certain polish, or social awareness. He wouldn't know crystal from glass, d'you know what I'm saying. He didn't know about etiquette and he was out of his depth at some of the social dos in Canberra. He never looked the part, even in uniform; looked more like a boilermaker or a fitter and turner, which he should have been.[16]

Knight tried to become a member of the circle of the army, but the subtleties of the unwritten tests defeated him.

REDEEMING MASCULINITY

Considering that murder has a function, what did Knight hope to achieve by his killing? Immediately after his arrest he repeated several times 'I have had military training', as if this was somehow an explanation or justification of his actions. And indeed for him it was, for Knight hoped to prove that he was a competent soldier by staging a real-life enactment of his skills. In his own accounts he speaks with what appears to be an utterly inappropriate pride in his use of cover so as not to be seen, his bringing down of the police helicopter, his coolness under fire by resting in a tree and smoking a cigarette during the police search of the area, and then, still according to the rules of the war going on in his head, surrendering to the enemy when he had run out of ammunition. His killings were designed to prove emphatically that the army was wrong in rejecting him.

There was a considerable overlay between his personal fantasy and the situation in which he found himself through the stress of the previous six months. He summed up his overall mental state as a perception that there was an 'invasion' going on

Murder

in Clifton Hill. Apart from his desire to become a war hero through some 'last stand', he was thus as much defending his own ego from impending disintegration through his killings as trying to prove his own suitability for the army. His reading of military history, in which he showed a predilection for sieges, merely fitted him well to turn suburban Clifton Hill into the battlefield on which he would redeem his masculinity.

Much has also been made of Knight's subsequent failure to show remorse. The code in which his remorse has been expressed is consistent with his enduring vision of himself as a soldier, necessary to his psychic survival, when he says '[T]he hardest thing to cope with is the fact that I gunned down people I had sworn to protect when I joined the army'.[17]

Vitkovic's and Knight's failure to form a sufficiently stable masculine identity drove them to take to the streets with their guns in order to prove their power in other devastating public ways by compensation. In doing so, they demonstrated how bankrupt of constructive ideas masculinity is when faced by a crisis. Frank Vitkovic said

> I've got a mental prison around me. That's the only way to describe it. There's no escape, no way out. It just gets worse and worse. Mental prisons are the worst.

The 'mental prison' he was talking about was the prison of blocked masculinity, but the man who says he has been backed into a corner has usually forced himself into that corner, and it is his masculinity that is keeping him there. He needs to see that the corner is of his own making, and that he has accepted its illusory walls. In the dead-end-speak of masculinity, if there is no apparent retreat or escape, the only response is violence.

The mass murderer will often demonstrate 'a kind of suicidal violence'.[18] The killer takes out his frustration at his blocked passage to manhood by killing others as well as the self; Wade Frankum and Frank Vitkovic finally killed themselves, and Julian Knight alleges he lost the bullet with which he intended to kill himself.

POWER, VIOLENCE AND INTIMACY

Criminologists have recognised that a more detailed approach is needed to the relationship between offender and victim in murder, the 'offender–victim pairing', as it is called. To call murder a 'dynamic social interaction'[19] makes us aware that the common idea of murder as a chance, spur-of-the-moment event, out of character on the part of the murderer, atypical of the relationship of murderer and victim, and followed by regret or remorse, is too simplistic. It is more fruitful to see murder as an event 'involving at least two actors in a social relationship that plays a dynamic role in the way that the homicide unfolds'.[20] When this approach is used, a clearer pattern of murder emerges. Murder as the action of a stranger, casual and unpremeditated, is replaced by a much more social view of murder as sited in networks of power and intimacy.

One category of murder that presents a clear view of men's insecurity and readiness to defend their role with lethal force is when a woman threatens to leave a relationship. In the figures for murder in Australia in 1990–91, the 'largest category of precipitating factor was that of altercation arising from jealousy or the termination of a sexual relationship, or the threat to do so'.[21] Indeed the theme of possessiveness, manifesting as 'an extreme sense of sexual jealousy'[22] and best summed up by one male offender's stated motivation 'If I can't have you, no one will', dominates the figures for murder in Victoria in 1985 and 1986.

A woman who leaves will not only ignite strong feelings in the man, but also re-ignite that original scene of separation which is so cataclysmic for a male — the rejection of the boy by the mother. The man will have learned early on that

> woman (as mother, carer, nurse, grandmother or teacher) is the primary source of all his most powerful feelings, good and bad. And a mother's place is in the wrong; for the rest of his life he will resent her power, either the power of her warmth (too engulfing, too reminiscent of his powerlessness), or the arctic winter of her coldness (too abandoning, too life-threatening).[23]

When the woman in a relationship threatens departure, perhaps taking the children with her, she is threatening to remove what the male perceives as his right: a network of respect with him at the centre, which is essential to his mental stability. When this is disturbed or removed he may respond with disproportionate force, for excessive force is typical of such scenarios. Women kill men with one blow or shot, as the 'single nature of the fatal wound'[24] frequently shows. Men, on the other hand, 'normally overkill women',[25] as shown by the 'multiple injuries observed in the male offender, female victim killings'[26] in Victoria in 1985 and 1986.

Men's violence as altercations escalate reveals their emotional inarticulacy, but this should come as little surprise, given that one of the main criteria of masculinity is that men be silent in the face of extreme emotion. That men erroneously hold women responsible as the cause of the emotional suffering during the turbulent ending of a relationship is indicated by the explanations they give after the event. To kill the woman is to end the pain. One murderer saw the death of his victim as an end to pain and the beginning of the peace of jail. 'I only wanted to destroy her . . . I wanted to get rid of her then I can go to jail and stay in peace.'[27]

William Towns, who slashed his estranged wife's throat aboard the Melbourne–Sydney express, gave as his explanation that 'I couldn't live with her, I couldn't live without her, so I had to end her'.[28] He was unable to deal with the strong emotion that their separation had caused.

Men need to be taking responsibility for their emotional state when the women with whom they are involved ask for independence. The question for men is not 'Why do you want to go?' directed at the woman, but 'Why can't I let her go?' directed at themselves.

There is that grotesque Australian insult, 'You're fucked in the head', which, if taken literally, could communicate the force with which men would like to invade women's minds. In David Ireland's radical vision of a future Australia in his novel *City of Women*, he projects the reader forward to a Sydney ruled by women, in which men are marginalised. There is on the loose a serial attacker called Old Man Death who at first merely attacks, knocks out or subdues his victim with chloroform, then makes an incision in the body, deposits his sperm in that incision, then sews it shut. Then a woman's heart is fucked. And finally a woman is found in a warehouse, the walls and beams hung with photographs of an attack on her.

> Each facet of the attack was shown; the saw tearing through the hair (no attempt was made to shave the head first and she had

Murder

waist-length hair); the circular saw biting through the scalp into the bone of the skull, throwing particles of bone like sawdust; the lifting off of the rounded top of the skull, the exposure of the brain; the sight of the strong penis, the first pressure against the soft brain tissue, the probing entry, the disappearance from sight of the major portion of the shaft of the penis into the grey matter, the hairy pubis pressed against the brain case . . . Semen was found planted deep in the brain.[29]

If, as the policewoman narrator remarks, 'nothing more horribly, more plainly against women could ever be done', it is because the assault graphically symbolises the urge shared by so many men to invade, possess and control women.

VIOLENCE BY MEN AGAINST MEN

Feminist lawyers and criminologists have done great service in drawing attention to rape, incest, child abuse and domestic violence in general. But to focus attention on the female victims of such crimes alone is to forget that gender also plays a part in violence by men against men. Though there may be a perception that women are numerically the greater number of victims of violent assault by men, it is worth remembering that 'for every woman who is violently assaulted, there are three or four men; for every 5,000 US female homicides in 1987, there were 15,000 male',[30] and Australia and Britain duplicate these ratios. While gender shows itself in attacks by men on women, it also shows itself in attacks by men on men. Though a brawl outside a western suburbs pub in Sydney might not be viewed as a gender-related event, the masculinity of the men involved is as much a factor as it would be in the rape of a woman at the same location, or a wife-battering when one of those men arrived home. Men are harming themselves and others in their acceptance of and readiness to use violence. The murder of men by men is also a product of gender; the men who murder other men are doing so from a complex set of motives to do with their masculinity, a related but subtly different set of motives as are present in the murder by men of women.

An American criminologist called Luckenbill has evolved a theory of 'confrontational homicide'. These murders are 'events involving a challenge and counter-challenge which leads to physical conflict'.[31] What is astounding in these situations is the trivial nature of the original challenge; it need not even be a direct slur or insult; it may be a matter as insignificant as someone wanting to sit on a seat on a train which someone else regards as theirs. In these murders 'the persistent problem of "face" or honour ... seem[s] ... to be quite helpful in understanding male to male confrontations'[32] and how they are resolved.

The most frequent site for confrontational murder is in or near licensed premises, and alcohol is well and truly implicated as a contributory factor. In nineteen of twenty-five confrontational murders in Victoria in 1985 and 1986 alcohol was a factor, and not in moderation, as the blood alcohol reading of some of the victims was 0.1 or more.[33]

The role of violence between males is the 'testing and establishment of power in relation to other men'.[34] After seventeen-year-old Jason Stuart had held the point of a knife fifteen centimetres from the throat of Ana Buchacher but had been dissuaded by his teacher from stabbing her he then sat down at a desk and wrote an explanation which was read out in court at his trial.

Murder

I decided that Ana must die to;
a) satisfy my revenge; and
b) to set an example to others that I can't be screwed around with.[35]

The first reason was the result of his perception that she had been 'stuffing him around', for which humiliation he was holding her responsible, and the second was to assert control, which he saw as necessary to his masculine identity.

The function murder performs for the murderer has been described as 'a defence against impending psychotic ego rupture', and 'episodic dyscontrol which functions as a regulatory device to forestall more extensive personality disintegration'.[36] Thus a possible role of murder for men is to defend the ego against what is perceived as imminent destruction. In this women risk the strongest retaliatory action because of their ability to deliver telling blows to a man's self-esteem, as do men who threaten a man's masculine self-image.

MISSING LINKS

That men are distant from themselves in killing is evident from their recounting of the events. John Glover, the 'Granny Killer', spoke of his murders 'as though he was telling a story about someone else'.[37] This distance from themselves, together with failure to give any emotional reality to those whom they kill, is at the heart of their actions. Close and real links with others allow a sense of interconnectedness that is vital to a sense of membership of community, for 'our sense of our humanity depends on feeling ourselves to be members of society, on having at least a few close relations with other human beings'.[38]

Junk Male

If those links are lacking, it seems that men care as little for themselves as they do for others. Even after killing they discover that it has not projected them into some more potent sense of themselves, but merely highlighted their own unbearable emptiness. When Wade Frankum had finished his killing in the Strathfield Plaza and was trying to escape, he realised 'he had come to a dead end with nothing but his own misery to show for it'.[39] He apologised to the woman whose car he tried to hijack — 'I'm sorry, I'm sorry' — then killed himself, cancelling his own life as he had cancelled seven other lives minutes before, leaving no statement but a myriad questions.

SUICIDE

What are the great sceptred dooms
To us, caught in the wild wave?
We break ourselves on them,
My brother, our hearts and years.

Isaac Rosenberg, 'On War'

My brother did no harm. His crime was thought and his punishment was death.

Shakespeare, *Richard II*

THE CATALYST

At about three-thirty in the afternoon of Friday 13 July 1973 my older brother fired a bullet from a .22 calibre rifle into his head, mortally wounding himself. He died in Royal Perth Hospital some three hours later. I was the last person to see him alive. When I arrived at the hospital shortly after his death my father took me in his arms with my mother and said: 'We shall always be four.'

I mention my brother's death at the outset because I must site it as an event in relation to the genesis and growth of the ideas in this book. My brother's death became for me the catalyst in all my thinking about masculinity. It became the touchstone against which all other experiences were judged, the yardstick of silently endured grief in the masculine world. All other losses and reverses could be explained away (I was a failure; I was 'not man enough'), but not his death. The pretence of objectivity in this chapter is just that; I am involved in this discussion by my underlying experience. I am present in these pages in an attempt to achieve insight and escape from the endless cycle of memory and mourning.

My brother's death is like an obsidian block which lies immovable in my life. It absorbs all light, and gives back none. Its centre is utterly dark and defeats all attempts at penetration. Yet it invites contemplation, which sometimes veers dangerously towards fascination. But I have not found a way to shatter it to its core so that I can be delivered from its intolerable weight.

Junk Male

The wound of my brother's death is the clearest sign through which I feel the contradictions of my gender. For all the years that pass there seems no cure. The stigmata of memory are perpetually there and will not film over with new surfaces. I cannot live, write, think or ignore it away. It is a question to which there is no answer. Through it I feel how fragile is my hold on my self and how fragile is my hold on life itself. It is the negative for every positive, the indifference behind every emotion, the despair behind every hope, the full stop at the end of every sentence.

It still takes me a good few seconds of mental arithmetic to work out how long it has been since my brother died. In the opposite way to mothers, who reckon time by births, I reckon time by a death: events are either before or after my brother's death. His death is in the past, eternally ago, and yet always the day before yesterday, the year before last, the recent event from which I am still recovering.

A PARTICULARLY MALE SOLUTION

My brother's death at twenty-one seems to me to reflect the difficulties involved in the transition from teenager to man, a transition he did not survive. His death is not atypical of the deaths of other boys seeking to become men in the fifteen to twenty-five age group, then and since. Male suicide has a second peak, though, and that is in the older than forty-five years group. This is when, as in late adolescence, there arise problems of transition from one phase of life to another. The older man's wife may have died, she may have left him in reaction to a life centred on his work, or she may simply have begun to demand some measure of autonomy in her life. There may be difficulties with

Suicide

teenaged children, whose increasing independence triggers buried envy and rage. The man may, as a result of any of these, find himself living alone, and facing loss and absence for the first time. Combined with the possibility of job insecurity, of 'outplacement' on an 'attractive early retirement package', the likelihood of some measure of alcohol dependence, and related or accidental illness or injury, you have a powerful mix of emotional distress and instability which may easily lead to suicide.

The question to be asking, then, is why suicide seems to have become such a particularly male solution to crises in times of transition and re-establishment of the self and its relationship to the world. Suicide is 'one of the last great male mysteries';[1] it is a problem that is uniquely ours as men, and we need to be interrogating ourselves about it in order to be better equipped to confront and inspect it.

Suicide presents problems of definition in coronial investigations into cause of death because there may be a considerable overlap between it and accidental death. Much adolescent male behaviour involves taking risks: accepting dares is a particularly male activity, even if those dares are directed by the individual against himself. The risks that many young men take seem suicidal, but rather than indicating a suicidal intention these actions indicate the extent to which an emerging teenage male will put his life on the line for his masculinity. To back down, to refuse the dare, is to lose masculine face at a time when to do so seems intolerable. Sometimes the dares are undertaken in the knowledge that to fail is to die, 'for example, jumping or swinging across a river or canal, when most of the boys, as working-class city kids, could not swim', or 'diving under a moving freight train and rolling out the other side with all your moving parts attached'.[2] As usual the site of the test must be one familiar to the participants, but made fearful by the unusual and dangerous action.

Such may have been the case with nineteen-year-old Tobias Adcock. The transit police said that he had been involved in graffiti and was likely to skylark on trains and 'gave the impression of being carefree and not worrying about the risks'.[3] Adcock fell off the 7.29 Glen Waverley train as it came out of the Melbourne Underground loop after having climbed onto the roof of the train to 'surf' it through the tunnels. The coroner, Mr McPherson, said in his summing up that 'if Mr Adcock's friends had encouraged him to do the stunt, they must live with the fact that they also contributed to his death'.

Such an accidental death poses questions as to why such an apparently suicidal risk should be taken. What such actions reveal, though, is the low value put on their lives by the young men who perform them. They throw their lives away casually through sheer carelessness, as if to dare God with their own mortality. Coroners have always tried to clearly and adequately define the line between accident and suicide by defining the difference as the presence of intention in some clear and categorical way, such as a letter or a degree of deliberation and premeditation in the means used. When there is doubt about the intention of the deceased, either an accidental or an open verdict is recorded; however, 'suicidal children rarely leave notes and some of their chosen modes of suicide — falling from heights, running into oncoming traffic, gun-shot wounding, motor vehicle accidents and drug overdose — may give rise to genuine confusion about intent'.[4]

Another aspect of the difficulty in assessing the accuracy of statistics on suicide is the coincidence of high rates of suicide and accidental death in the same age groups, especially the

Suicide

fifteen to nineteen age group for males. More than fifty per cent of motorcycle accidents, for example, are in the fifteen to twenty-five age group for men. But whether or not the statistics on suicide are blurred by an overlap with accidental death, what suicide and accidents reveal is that young men have a very casual attitude to their own lives, and are prepared to throw them away as much from despair over an impossible personal crisis as in a momentary surge of bravado before their peers or when alone.

What emerges from an analysis of men's responses to stress is that it appears difficult to gauge what the target of male frustration and despair will be, the self or others. Thus the casual way in which men act towards their mortality is doubly of concern. There seems no reliable way of predicting whether a man will implode (that is, select himself as the target of his frustration and stress) and suicide, or explode and select others as targets, even though this violence may include an intention to die sufficiently clear to be called suicidal.

This difficult difference can best be explored by looking at the death of Geoff Whyte in Wagga Wagga.[5] Though Whyte was twenty-one and unemployed, football had given direction to his life; he had been part of the premiership-winning Wagga Saints team in 1991, and there was talk of his being signed to play with a Melbourne club. Then his weight fell from 76 to 57 kilograms, and he was diagnosed as having pericarditis. He became depressed and let friendships lapse until, according to his football coach, he had become 'a recluse'. He would play heavy-metal music for several nights in a row, and his mother could not get him to stop. His confidante and best friend, Marion Knobel, could not talk him out of his depressed state.

He stole a 12-gauge shotgun and a white Commodore sedan, actions utterly unusual for him, and drove to the

McPherson Oval, where his team had won the premiership the previous year. He turned the car's headlights onto high beam and fired shots into the air to attract the attention of the police who, when they arrived, switched on the oval's floodlights and tried to negotiate with Whyte. Though he seemed to calm down — walking around the oval with the gun held down rather than up — when at last he met police in a poorly lit area behind the change-room after a seven-hour stand-off he made as if to shoot by raising his shotgun and was shot by an armed officer, the bullet glancing off his elbow into his chest. He died almost instantly.

THE DISINTEGRATING MALE

There are a number of high-risk characteristics of suicide:[6] being older than forty-five, male, white; being widowed, separated, or divorced; living alone; being unemployed or retired; physical illness especially of a chronic nature; mental disorder, including alcohol dependence; previous suicide attempts; and medical care within the previous six months. A person with all these characteristics would present several hundred times more risk of suicide during the following years. When some form of depressive illness and intense hopelessness and neglect are added to the above profile, that male has entered a difficult and dangerous period.

The age group in the above set of characteristics is a reflection of the second peak of suicidal behaviour by men after the age of forty-five, but it has emerged that being between fifteen and twenty-five is also a high-risk period for men. Once age has been set aside it is clear that Geoff Whyte shared several of the factors: he was male, white and unemployed, and had a severe illness of a chronic nature which meant that he had

Suicide

had detailed medical attention over the previous months, and though he was not living alone and had a significant confidante with whom he was still communicating, it is possible that he experienced a degree of social isolation as a result of his need to be seen as masculine and to give the appearance of coping.

It could also be said, as observed in the chapter on murder, that the factors indicated as being characteristic of a suicidal situation are also those which seem to characterise the potential for explosion of mass murderer. Frank Vitkovic, for example, was twenty-two years old, white, male and unemployed, and had had a prolonged physical illness that prevented him from playing tennis, his favourite sport, to which he attached a lot of importance. In the chapter on murder the suicidal intent of the mass murderer was discussed, and this must have been the dilemma facing the police negotiators as they dealt with Whyte: what were his motives in taking the car and the gun, going to that public place only five hundred metres from his home and then drawing attention to his being there by firing shots and putting the car's headlights on high beam? Were they faced with a potential suicide or murderer? Had he returned to the oval to attempt some connection with a personal success, where just months before he had listened as the crowd cheered his team in triumph, or was he making the last stand typical of the disintegrating male? Either way, it seems that when a man's masculinity is threatened by circumstances which put it under stress, then a man will put his own life or the lives of others at risk.

This fact has ramifications for health professionals who are likely to come into contact with such males, as the diagnostic model for the suicidal may need to take into account the possibility of an explosion of violence aimed at others. If the suicidal patient is tested for 'the past response to stress, especially loss; the tolerance of disturbing affects such as rage or self-contempt; the means of handling aggression; the degree of impulse control; the capacity for reality testing; the quality of relationship with significant others; the availability of a suitable method for suicide'[7] — which in the case of men will mean their (preferred means) guns may also be used to kill others, then this test could also take into account the possibility of murderous intent as well.

Geoff Whyte's death draws attention to the pressures that Australian men face in their transition from boyhood to manhood. The death rate from suicide in the fifteen to nineteen age group in rural municipalities and shires in New South Wales, where Geoff Whyte lived, increased dramatically from 1964 to 1988, outstripping urban Sydney rates; rural rates rose five-fold, while urban rates only two-fold.[8] The relatively clear social picture of rural life and values may help to elucidate some of the pressures typical of those that all Australian boys must face in negotiating their way into manhood.

The background of rural Australia in the last twenty-five years has been one of steady decline and mounting economic pressure as overseas markets have shrunk, farms have consolidated, and small business has collapsed.[9] This has caused high unemployment, and as so much of a man's vision of himself is occupationally based, men have suffered the most serious erosion of self-esteem in their apparent inability to support themselves through consistent work. A study in Australia has now replicated numerous overseas studies which indicate that unemployment is felt first and most seriously by men, who respond with catastrophic consequences for themselves.[10] In extreme situations of unemployment such as the Great Depression, Australian male suicide rates reached their highest levels ever.[11]

Suicide

If unemployment in itself is a significant factor in male suicide, it might be logical to assume that male suicide would fall in times of stability or economic growth. However, this corollary does not occur. Whether in the boom years of the 1960s, or in the 1980s when inflation and unemployment rose steadily, male suicide rates have continued to rise whether the economy was in a state of boom or one of slump. This seems to support Durkheim's view that whenever there are 'disturbances of the collective order' men are the most immediate casualties: 'Whenever serious re-adjustments take place in the social order, whether or not due to sudden growth or to an unexpected catastrophe, men are more inclined to self-destruction'.[12] This runs counter to the fondly held image of Australian men as 'battlers' who 'cope' when the 'going gets tough'. To the contrary, men seem to be acutely sensitive to disturbance in their occupationally based view of the world, whether it be in the form of depressions that create pressure to retain jobs and the role of bread-winner, or booms when the pressures are to achieve appropriate levels of success.

The departure of the son from the rural home may be a more traumatic and less assured time than a similar event in an urban setting. It is possible to 'speculate that stressed rural families may place pressure on adolescents to leave home at an earlier age and perhaps in more critical circumstances than their urban counterparts'.[13] When the son leaves home the options for social activity or tertiary or further education are limited, and when there are problems of access and confidentiality with appropriate health facilities, then an already difficult passage becomes even more arduous, and 'life transition problems'[14] multiply. Faced by urban and global forces affecting the economy in such a way that comprehension is defeated and male self-reliance is nearly impossible, and by the cultural view that 'mental illness [is] to be seen as a moral failing',[15] the rural Australian male is caught in a bind of trying to live up to a dated ideal, achievement of which is becoming steadily more improbable, and for which the price of failure is despair and death.

SEPARATION FROM LIVING

Suicide also demonstrates the way in which men are not meaningfully linked to those about them in society. To return to the original criteria for suicide if being widowed, divorced or separated and living alone are factors in male suicide, then men seem less able to weather the period of adjustment immediately after separation. Thus suicide seems to indicate that men have not achieved as profound a sense of connectedness within society, as much 'social integration',[16] as women have. In the first sixty years of this century, for example, one researcher found a 'complete absence of any female suicides among the single, the separated, and the divorced outside the metropolitan area of Perth'[17] in Western Australia. The wilful social isolation of the male suicide, in which all contact with friends is curtailed or stopped completely, seems to be a dramatic pointer to the male's perceived social distance from human contact at other times as well as immediately prior to the act of suicide.

In male suicide it seems that some great doubt shears through life like a geological fault and separates the man from living. When circumstances combine to rupture a man's sense of himself and the continuity of his emotional life and existence, then he will be prone to suicidal impulses, for his life seems at an end and he does not have the resources to re-establish a sense

Suicide

of time and his presence in it, or the future in any meaningful sense. As Boris Pasternak commented:

> [A] man who decides to commit suicide puts a full stop to his being, he turns his back on his past, he declares himself a bankrupt and his memories to be unreal. They can no longer help or save him, he has put himself beyond their reach. The continuity of his inner life is broken, his personality at an end.[18]

If one of the effects of being brought up to be male is alienation from self and others, an alienation even from the body as a source of sensory calm, and a deep-rooted inarticulacy about emotions, their sources and causes — in short a lack of connection to self and others — then when circumstances combine to create a moment of real perception of that distance, nothing can stand against the implosive forces which would be released by that moment. There will be no link to self or others that will act as a lifeline to keep that man in the world. The utter despair and the rejection of all things are apparent as the final balance is drawn. The world of the suicide seems more likely to be a male world. If 'suicide is a closed world with its own irresistible logic',[19] the detachment from the world which allows departure from it is particularly male.

While the period in which the suicidal matrix emerges may vary from days to a few weeks even months, it seems that there is nothing that can break through the introverted, introjected logic of the male ego. When at last the final challenge comes, it will come 'like all the other key moments of men's lives, in silence and pain'.[20] In this the attitude of the suicide again resembles the frame of mind of the murderer, as everything in the world is interpreted in the light of the central drive, and nothing is allowed to be positive or to deflect the mind from its morbid task. Everything confirms the drive towards death.

If in the murder of women by men the recurring phrase is 'If I can't have you no-one will', with the suicide of men the repeated puzzles posed by the stunned survivors are: 'Why did he do it?'; 'He never said anything'; 'He seemed to have everything to live for'. The first of these can be answered adequately, even though for the living the reasons never seem to add up to sufficient cause to end a life. The second is predictable, given men's need to project an aura of coping. A life-and-death decision will be taken without reference to anyone else, and then carried out. The third? It must be realised that the fragility of a man's emotional understanding is such that no link to another person or possession of material things will keep a man in life, for none of those links or desires has any reality to a man in a suicidal frame of mind.

Those men who have weathered the transition into adulthood and established a more mature masculine identity and therefore seem to 'have something to live for', the male suicides in or around their forties, still kill themselves.

> A highly successful solicitor, a former mayor of Beaconsfield and owner of a 50,000 pound Maserati, among other good things of life, Hugh Simmonds apparently had everything to live for. Although married he was planning a holiday with the woman with whom he had been having a long-standing affair, whose parents later said that the couple had been very much in love. Shortly before they were due to leave, Simmonds was found dead in his car from carbon monoxide poisoning.[21]

Suicide

Australian men seem to be no exception. The people of Kilmore where the Knight family had their stables 'were left with a question that may never be answered' when Vin Knight killed himself in 1991 at the age of thirty-six, for 'on the surface at least he seemed to have everything to live for'.[22] He was a successful reinsman, holding a number of records for the total number of winners in a season, and even at that stage of the season had driven so many winners that he was posthumously awarded Reinsman of the Year. When Floyd Podgornik killed himself at the age of forty-nine in the St Kilda Road Melbourne offices of his own company, Podgor, there were rumours of financial improprieties, though subsequent examination revealed no such problems in his business empire. The father of two sons, with a wife and mistress, owner of the famed Melbourne restaurant Florentino's, as well as racehorses at the Symbol Lodge stud and a black turbo-charged Bentley, he was well known and well liked by his workers, and 'lived the good life [with] fast cars, [and was] a flashy gambler. Until, without apparent reason, he shot himself'.[23] Constable Grant Eastes was one of the first policemen on the scene of the Grafton bus crash in New South Wales in 1989, where 'composed (looking nonetheless far in excess of his 29 years of age) he spoke of the carnage relatively unemotionally'.[24] A brave officer, he had been decorated for arresting an armed bank robber. The question over his death was '[W]hy, with a wife and two lovely daughters, did a bright ambitious 29-year-old take his life in a lonely motel room?' It seems that no link between any of these men and other people or things was sufficient to hold them to life.

In times of transition and stress in the late teens and early twenties, and then again later in life, roughly after forty years of age, men suffer a degree of turbulence against which they have few means of resistance. 'In youth and age, then, at key times of insecurity and transition, men find it harder to hold on to their sense of self and purpose, easier to reach for the false certainty of the terminal conclusion which provides them with a solution no matter what the cost to anyone else.'[25] When faced with a crisis of identity and direction, men seem ill-equipped to respond in creative ways and create a new self which can better fit in and benefit from the changing circumstances of their lives, or the society around them. Instead they demonstrate fatally rigid patterns of thought which lead to the cul-de-sac of death.

An accepted cost of masculinity?

Suicide as a response to the crises of life seems to be becoming a progressively earlier response for males: it is alarming to note that 'suicide has been increasingly slipping into the younger age groups', and that 'the magnitude of the problem is very serious among teenage males'[26] in Australia. As society presents an increasingly alluring picture of autonomy and independence to the young, and while young men increasingly strive towards it, so the friction with authority figures increases, as well as the impression that life is running too slowly towards their acquiring that all-important label, 'man'. If 'the young have formal "rights" but the autonomy to exercise these rights is mediated by parental and societal approval, and in some instances such approval may not be granted either by parents or society',[27] then they will experience a severe sense of social disruption in their life-path towards masculine adulthood.

The statistics are stark indicators of an epidemic in male deaths by suicide in Australia, no matter how they are analysed by age group or year bracket. The national rate for males in the

Suicide

fifteen to nineteen age group has doubled in the last twenty-one years,[28] and going further back, has trebled over the last thirty years.[29] In a curious mirror of statistics, men in all age groups outnumber women in suicide by the same proportion, three to one, as they do as victims of murder.[30] In an interesting change in a formerly well-established pattern, young males have also been attempting suicide more frequently; for the fifteen to nineteen age group the hospital admission rate for males as a result of attempted suicide increased by 114 per cent when the rates for 1971–72 and 1986–87 were compared, while female rates increased by six per cent.[31] In the past thirty years, while rates for females have increased, they have not done so as dramatically; they have increased at a rate consistent with population increase or the percentage of the female population at risk; or in some decades they have been stable. Even so the highest rate for female suicide, 10.8 per 100 000 in 1965, was still barely higher than the lowest male rate of 9.9 per 100 000 in 1944.[32]

If any other group in Australian society was dying at such a rate, and that rate was steadily rising, then action might be taken, but if they are men and they are dying it seems to say that such deaths are just an accepted cost of masculinity. The value of male life needs to be rediscovered: '[N]o society which values its individual members can permit its males to go on damaging and killing themselves.'[33]

As it is we seem to have 'no scientifically defensible model to explain suicide',[34] nor is there a recognition that male suicide is a 'major public health issue'.[35] If 'the causes of suicidal behaviour in young persons remain enigmatic . . . [then] so too do the appropriate measures to combat it'.[36] Part of the problem in dealing with male suicide is the reluctance of men to recognise themselves as being at risk. 'A trap for suicide prevention programs may be forgetting those who are least visible. It is widely recognised that men attend psychiatric services less frequently than women.'[37]

> [While] in recent years medical and social agencies have become more available for women in emotional distress such services may be more tuned to the needs of females than males. Thus while the so-called 'epidemic' of attempted suicide in females appears to have been arrested, the situation for males may have been overlooked.[38]

The act of suicide dramatically draws attention to the burden of doubts that men carry, which at moments of crisis may suddenly appear to accumulate to the point where they appear unbearable, and to be insuperable barriers between the present and the future. This is particularly true for young men like my brother, as 'young males on the brink of manhood have all too often failed the final transition to manhood, and have chosen instead the last great leap into the dark'.[39] The strength of response of men to the suicide of other men might seem to indicate that such an option is never far from any man's mind.

Returning to my brother's death, I have found out how 'the suicide assists passively at the cancellation of his own history, his work, his memories, his whole inner life — in short, of everything that defines him as an individual'.[40] There are diaries and photographs, but the main burden of recall falls on my memory, and I wish to speak from that memory before he fades from existence, and is lost utterly and forever. And that utter annihilation is what I seek to defeat by speaking of the pain that

Suicide

sent him silently to his death and the pain that has endured in me. I wanted to speak from the silent room within of an 'absence, a silence, a loss at the heart'[41] which informs my masculine view of the world. If his death was the first silence for me, in writing this book I shall make the breaking of that silence the last word.

CONCLUSION

We are born, so to speak, twice over; born into existence, and born into life; born a human being, and born a man . . . and this critical moment, short enough in itself, has far-reaching consequences.

Rousseau, *Emile*

We all carry within us our places of exile, our crimes and our ravages, but our task is not to unleash them on the world; it is to fight them, in ourselves and in others.

Camus, *The Rebel*

Reshaping masculinity

The focus of this book has been on the narratives that men use to give shape to their lives, the constant battles that men have to absorb and identify with masculine tradition, and how they damage themselves and others in the process. Much of men's energies is spent unproductively in conforming to the demands of masculinity, and so they themselves remain unavailable in any meaningful way to those around them. Men may invest so much in the masculine style to which they subscribe that they are unable to see how it traps them, even as it holds out illusory promises of freedom. Because men are trapped within a narrow range of masculine behaviours, their actions perpetuate oppressive relationships in society because men are preoccupied with justifying themselves and their actions within the limits of masculinity. The result is mere repetition in ignorance, and the limitations to action imposed by masculine codes are passed from one generation of men to the next.

Internalised narratives are lifelines around which men organise their lives into sequences of events. This allows men to achieve the self-mastery necessary to successful masculinisation. But this 'mastery is achieved by clinging to narratives and to linear time, evading those spaces which threaten fusion and the loss of self'.[1] In the men's biographies and autobiographies I have referred to there are few that actually recognise that feminism has occurred, and fewer authors who grapple with it in any detail. The impact of feminism is avoided as men retreat into the stable social landscape of the immediate post-war years. Thus autobiography allows an escape into the past; 'nostalgia replaces the imperfect present with a perfect past'[2] in which there is no discord and women are not problematical presences, made threatening by enhanced self-assertion. One woman reviewer of a number of such autobiographies said that she was tired of the world they presented,

> [a] male fantasy world without women apart from Mum and Gran. A world of blokes and beer and footy and emotional mateship; of backyard cricket with Dad and the brothers, punch-ups in pubs, deep discussions on Art and Life over the joints, and hippie journeys. 'Australia' is the stubble-chinned, beer and tobacco-smelling old men in stained raincoats.[3]

Increasingly it seems that the successful mastery of masculinisation can be achieved only in retrospective narratives.

One of the effects of feminism that men might welcome is that the continuity of men's narratives has been irrevocably broken. If men try to live their lives by outdated models, then women will draw attention to it. If in dealing with women today men experience 'a disparity between their lived relations and their inherited languages of masculinity',[4] then that disjunction should be welcomed as a chance to reassess masculinity and reshape it into new forms.

Masculinity is not something for which there is still a set pattern, a set of rules, which if followed slavishly will bestow manhood. The overall picture is getting harder and harder to detect, the clear examples harder and harder to discern. 'I've begun to wonder if life is something like collecting jigsaw puzzle pieces with no boxes', muses one middle-aged man,

Conclusion

so you're never too sure if you should be making one picture or several different ones. Lots of pieces don't seem to quite fit together, yet I think you tell yourself the picture looks right, right enough for the time being. But there always seems to be that little whispering uncertainty, and somehow never less than a couple of handfuls of bits left over that don't appear to go anywhere. And every now and then you collect up a whole heap of new ones.[5]

Not even fathers are any help in this, as when the man's father dies, he 'is finished with his collection of pieces now. He made whatever pictures he could from them, and moved on, and left them to me'.[6] When ten years old, on a long car journey, the son listened as his father and an uncle discussed their lives, which had been disrupted by the Second World War

> not with bitterness, not as innocent bystanders should, drawn away as they were into a vortex of angry governments, that took over their smallest and most private of circumstances. They reflected instead on the altered courses of their life histories, and mostly with resignation, some pride of achievement, a touch of regret.
>
> Yet, only looking back now do I understand they spoke as if still unsure of the context, as if it were still too soon, but feeling compelled to grope for perspective.[7]

The small boy in the back gathered up their observations avidly, with his 'infinite need to follow, to construct some kind of understanding'.[8] His account ends with an assertion that he will throw himself into the remaining time allotted to him and become active in shaping his future: 'I have this feeling that a circle of time is forming, my own, I must begin again, today, at the beginning, and refashion its direction, before it closes.'[9]

To do this will require courage and independence, not a readiness to return to earlier models based on a nostalgia for certainties. Men need to be careful not to fall into the trap of envying those whose masculine codes are apparently simpler and clearer.

Dilemmas reflected in male narratives

The evidence for this book was drawn from biography, autobiography, and fiction by and about men. The reason for this was that whether men are writing directly about themselves or other men in biography, or indirectly in fiction, they wittingly or unwittingly reveal the masculine style by which they live, and the masculine style they most admire. However, the effect of masculinisation in male biography needs to be examined, because if it reflects the internalised narratives by which men order their lives then the outmoded masculine forms and men's recurring dilemmas will be apparent. There are typical narrative profiles that men use. 'The plot [of male autobiographies] borrowed from the *Odyssey*, shows us the narrator being tested in an heroic journey, emerging victorious from his trials, ready to claim his rightful place and his faithful Penelope.'[10] The exactitude with which Bert Facey's *A Fortunate Life* followed this plot might explain its popularity. Facey survived early physical tests alone in foster families and later as a jackeroo; he enlisted, fought at Gallipoli, and then returned to Australia and married happily. The almost exact overlap between the events in Facey's life and the life of Australia as a nation may also have contributed to the warmth with which Australian readers responded to the book.

Conclusion

In conforming to this essential plot, however, the narrator's attention will be limited by his concentration on the values of masculinity with which he has struggled, either assimilating and accommodating them, or being rejected by and rejecting them. Certainly the impression that could be formed from reading Australian male biographies since the Second World War is of a masculine culture which is a 'strongly authoritarian society, intolerant of human difference, timidly conventional, highly class conscious, thoroughly materialistic and utilitarian in its values, and either distrustful or positively hostile to the arts'.[11] While any autobiography will inevitably deal with the tensions between the individual and society, it seems that Australian men are caught up with outward events, social analysis and competition for status at the expense of the inner life. Women autobiographers are more perceptive and receptive in this area.

If the biographies of men show the struggle of the individual male with society to achieve some kind of adult status, their narratives also reveal their battles to become masculine. Men struggle with the question of whether they should follow the approved codes of masculinity, or strike out in some truly independent direction of being. When Clive James asks in *Unreliable Memoirs*, the first volume of his autobiography, 'which was I, a conformist or a nonconformist?',[12] he is asking himself whether he wants to join in the construction of a typical masculine self, or whether he wants to take off on some utterly different project of self. The narrative of his life details his vacillation between the extremes of juvenile larrikinism and adolescent virtue. In his account of his prevarication he veers from smug self-satisfaction at getting the cane because of the 'fame accruing to the maximum penalty', to how he saw becoming class captain as a 'clear endorsement of my personality and attainments',[13] and boasting of how he 'was privileged, in my capacity as prefect, to book [the "greatest male swimmer on earth" John Konrads] for running in the playground'[14] at Sydney Technical College.

What might influence James to swing from one extreme to the other is the connection between behaviours associated with power, which are preferable to those behaviours that go unrewarded. As James simply sums it up, 'I was very keen not to be among the victimised. It followed that I should become one of those doing the victimising'.[15] James reveals that he used laughter as a means of avoiding scrutiny. He says 'one of the reasons I grew up feeling the need to cause laughter was perpetual fear of being its unwitting object'.[16] The harsh laughter directed at the outcasts from the male circles of power in the classroom was what spurred James to discover ways in which he could direct the laughter away from himself at some other target. Throughout his account of discovering the power of directed laughter to protect the self from scrutiny James constantly harps on his estimate of his self-worth. Most of the time he oscillates from self-aggrandisement and vanity to the most abject self-castigation. It seems that his readiness to seek humour has clouded and obscured any accuracy of self-perception, and James' humour highlights the crisis of value of the male self. Humour, observed in others or created in the self, is where some men in autobiography 'seek and find refuge; whether it be nervous and sardonic, witty and satiric, [humour is] the sanctioned province of "good form" for "good fellows", the great escape route from confrontation with the totality of self'.[17]

So often what we see in male autobiography is a crisis of value, and the many obstructions that masculinity places between a man and an accurate perception of himself. 'I have

Conclusion

always disliked myself at any given moment; the total of such moments is my life', Cyril Connolly breezily begins his autobiography; 'the first occurred on the morning ... when I was born.'[18] Men are brought up to feel 'different', 'exceptional' and 'unique', but at the same time their experiences convince them they are anonymous, lost in a vast and faceless mass. Neither proposition allows men much real commerce with themselves or others; uniqueness sets us apart, and anonymity denies others as well as ourselves any humanity. Thus men are 'always living out the dilemma between being "exceptional" and being "worthless"'.[19] Men are not encouraged to have a balanced view of themselves and their place in society. Such a contradiction runs through the first volume of Clive James' autobiography. Vaulting arrogance and self-abasement follow each other with bewildering rapidity and James' claims to self-knowledge are to be greeted with scepticism.

CONTAINMENT OF EMOTION IN AUTOBIOGRAPHY

While one of the conventions of autobiography is that the reader will be told an authentic story, based on an honest recall of crucial events in the protagonist's life, this is rarely the case in male autobiography. The reality of the emotions described by men in autobiography must be questioned, for what does emerge is not so much what was felt, but what was not felt, or what was felt but not expressed. For the containment of emotion so that the masculine persona of the narrator remains intact, rather than flowing out into the world, is very much at the heart of male autobiography. Thus what we see in autobiography is not so much revelation, but concealment within the conventions of the genre. To a man, writing is:

an exercise in emotional repression, about the way in which the suppression of self has been enforced by puritanical lip-service to the doctrine of 'objectivity', the cult of manliness, and how the language of nurture and spontaneous imaginative creativity has been consequently impoverished.[20]

In Australian male autobiography the urge for direct statement of feeling is constantly at odds with the nervous watchfulness of masculinity, which means that any display of feeling has to be defended, even derided, in order to prevent the reader from forming the view that the writer was making a direct emotional statement, or considered himself of importance. Relentless self-censorship is a problem ; it is as if the male author wanted the reward of self-display without the attendant cost. Despite the bravado, there is 'an underlying need to evade too close a confrontation with the self'.[21]

When the urge for self-expression meets the need to be masculine, can expression win out? What happens when the urge to reveal collides head-on with the urge to conceal? This may be behind the eternal self-watchfulness betrayed by so many of the most sophisticated of Australian male autobiographers. In Hal Porter's *The Watcher on the Cast-Iron Balcony* there seems to be a desire on Porter's part to evade emotional responsibility as well as emotional display by presenting a suitably neutral masculine mask:

> Because I am in my best clothes, in public, and an unknown place, I wish to commit the lie of manliness and impassivity while, at the same time, committing the lie of being a happy-go-lucky child not really aware of what is going on, and therefore not subject to emotional disarrangement.[22]

Conclusion

Hal Porter's lie to others, that he is a 'happy-go-lucky child', spills over into a lie to the self in order that he should avoid the emotional impact of what is going on around him, with his parents and their conflicting and contradictory demands on him. The self-consciousness of the watcher of self is revealed as being in opposition to deep discovery of the self.

Alan Moorehead encountered the same problem in recalling his life at Scotch College, where he was academically weak.

> I do not like being at the bottom of the class. I hate it. It fills me with shame and resentment. There are other stupid boys but somehow they manage to get by and most of them are bigger and faster on their feet than I am, and they find a place in the cricket teams in summer and the football teams in winter — a thing I can never hope to do. And so I am a withdrawn and rather sullen little boy.[23]

When he asks his sister for her view of him during those years, however, she says that on the contrary, he was a 'cheerful little boy, and although I did not do very well at my lessons I was bright as a button'. As Moorehead then asks: '[W]here is truth? If my sister is right then I must have been a mighty self-pitier and self-deceiver.'

But there is more: '[E]ither that, or I must have learned, even at that early age, the value of setting up a facade between myself and the world, an outward show of confidence that was designed to mask my weakness and uncertainty.' Has Moorehead's sister been taken in by his facade of being 'bright as a button'? Or is Moorehead's memory still the authentic view? Who has deceived whom? The path back to a true self becomes complex and baffling.

Junk Male

MASCULINE NARRATIVES IN FICTION

The dominance of men's lives by masculine narratives is also apparent in fiction written by men. In their novels men create characters who have great difficulties in relinquishing their preferred ways of telling and being. Cliff Hardy, Peter Corris' detective narrator, is one example. The first name itself is strongly evocative; it is 'a naturalised form of vertiginous endurance', as one critic has pointed out,[24] combining hardness, durability, impassivity and the inflexibility of the cliff's edge. The basic form of the detective thriller is the 'structure of threat and resolution; what is the crime or the set of crimes; what is the set of values, usually embodied in the hero, which are shown to resolve this threat?' In resolving this threat the hero of the detective thriller must be an 'archetype of bourgeois man; skilled, urban, isolated, fee-earning, suspicious, anxious, morally tired, adjective loving'.

In an interview Peter Corris defined the origin of Cliff Hardy as 'an older generation of Australians — uncles, father's friends, men who came back from the war. They are strong and not really silent, tough rather than rough, deeply imbued with a colloquial sense of rectitude' and they value 'persistence, courage, cunning and egalitarian good sense'. The opening of the novel *Matrimonial Causes* shows how Cliff Hardy eternally presents himself in character. Cliff and his latest woman friend, Glen Withers, are relaxing while on holiday.

'Good holiday, eh?'
   'Terrific.'
   'Did you have any good holidays with Cyn?'
   I tried to remember. I'd been married to Cyn for eight years. We must have had some holidays, but I couldn't recall any. No recession back then — maybe we'd been too busy

Conclusion

> detecting and architecting. I shook my head. 'None come to mind.'
>
> 'With Helen Broadway?'
>
> More recent history — a battlefield, essentially. 'If you can call Hastings a holiday, or Agincourt, or Dien Bien Phu. I went to New Caledonia with a woman once. We had a pretty good time.'
>
> 'And where's she now?'
>
> Ailsa Sleeman. 'She died of cancer a few years back.'
>
> 'Did you love her?'
>
> 'Glen, what is this?'
>
> 'I feel like talking. No, I feel like listening. How long have you been a private detective, Cliff?'
>
> ''Bout twenty years.'
>
> 'Gee, I was still at school when you started.'
>
> 'Yeah, in Year Twelve.'
>
> Glen laughed. 'Not quite. Tell me about your first case. You must remember it.'[25]

This exchange shows how Hardy's memory operates. He chooses not to remember; he has no clear memory of any holiday, good or bad, with a woman. How might Glen feel about such a revelation? Hardy also seems to resent questions; as a detective, it is his role to ask the questions, and others to answer. His past, though, seems a deliberate blank; to recall it is to summon up death, defeat and separation. In terms of form, the subsequent narrative is a dramatic monologue told to Glen Withers. While the relaxing setting, the holiday and the warmly appreciative and sympathetic audience might be expected to contribute to a different mode of narrative, what we hear is the same relentlessly minimalist masculine tale of daring and action.

Once again, the 'firm narrative curves' of the genre have set boundaries to the extent of self-revelation.

Working towards our own masculine forms

In reviewing the experiences of men put forward in this book, it might be expected that a conclusion would consist of a series of specific suggestions as to what men could do and what men might become, but I will resist the temptation to put forward any list. I do not intend to prescribe, because to do so is to proscribe. Having looked at the way in which masculinity is created and functions in many circumstances, I realise any attempt to suggest a particular set of values to which men might aspire, or any course of action to be followed, would be counter-productive, because it would once again aim behaviour at certain patterns of action and in turn create new guidelines for masculine style. Each man should be working towards his own masculine forms, even though that will bring him into conflict with the people around him, whose interests lie in having that man do what is expected of him within former limits. What any man is doing in order to be male is enough, whether that is being a ballet dancer, singing in an *a capella* choir, playing sport, drinking with friends, or all of those things. David Tacey, a speaker on men's issues, is frequently asked about such masculine forms:

> When I conduct courses or seminars on masculinity I am always asked for a prescriptive account of the New Male. I instinctively step back from this request and try to address the anxiety that underlies it. Many men, rather than attempting to find their own individual style, simply want to be told how to act, how to behave and how to think. The idea of a New Male

Conclusion

is potentially dangerous, not only because it is prescriptive but because it is singular. If it were to gain momentum in the social sphere it could well become dictatorial, hardly better than the old patriarchal stereotype that it replaces. Men have to be made aware that there is no one way in which they could be said to be 'real men', or 'truly masculine'.[26]

A possible aim might be towards achieving a comfortable balance that leads to the true calm of personal equilibrium, because then and only then can we begin to make decisions, rather than being forced into action by what we perceive to be the threats, encroachments, or example of others. It is not that we need to be like some exemplary male; we need to be more like ourselves, thus creating more ways of being masculine, a multitude of masculinities. There needs to be more room for sexual dissidence and variety in Australian society.

Rick, a character in Michael Gow's play *Away*, sums up what can happen if a man allows his life to become dominated by form and example:

> I'm just going round the twist, I think. I do things I don't understand. I have a job I don't want. I got married and I can't remember why. I'm going to buy a house and I can't remember why ... I'm going to end up in a strait-jacket. Everything I do is wrong. But I can't help myself. I just do things and I don't see why.[27]

The antidote to such a profound sense of inauthenticity is Nietzsche's command to 'be yourself! Everything you are doing, thinking, wanting is not really you!'[28]

Men must learn to speak with a new 'I', not a threatened, dictatorial 'I', which sees the world as having been structured for its benefit, but a far more modest 'I', in which voice, without hatred or rancour, we ask for a recognition of our difficulties and the need for us to begin a long journey towards some kind of enlightenment from which we might be able to look back at past thoughtlessness with a rueful smile.

If we listen to ourselves carefully we will detect and admit those moments at which we begin to project ourselves onto the world with the mix of anger born of fear which characterises the threatened male. Too often, in the rush to become masculine we ignored those moments at which we felt a degree of strain between ourselves and the role we were struggling to assimilate into our repertoire. Those moments, full of anxiety at being adrift from any role of clear power, are perhaps the best guide to us now. If we can site ourselves in those moments, but not cling desperately to previous outmoded models of behaviour, we can realise that our options are wider than we might have thought and make choices that are more conducive to more reasonable outcomes. Masculinity is to do with narrowed options, which means that we are pushed by models and examples that we believe it is worthwhile to become, rather than considering broader ranges of behaviour: a man has not 'gotta do what a man's gotta do'.

Our failure to create ways of being that are congenial to us is a reflection on our inability to see beyond established ways of perceiving masculinity. Robert Dessaix could say that he had been

> brought up to see life as linear, sequential and consequential, as heroic or tragic, modelled ideally, perhaps, on Jesus of Nazareth's or less loftily on any adventurer's. Yet deep down I know that a life can be pictured, construed, made sense of in terms of a completely different geometry altogether.[29]

Conclusion

His book, *A Mother's Disgrace*, is the account of his exploration of other adjacent, parallel, differently shaped worlds, which are merely a matter of a readiness to conceive of different curves, planes and boundaries. The only limit to entry is the ability to imagine such geometries.

Past moments of role strain that might be called displacement will be clearer, moments at which, in transition from one state to another, there was a sense of being outside both, and thus being able to see the two from a distance. This moment, no matter how fleeting, if recalled accurately, might form the basis for a reconsideration of one's life, because that moment of displacement was a moment of great potential. One's life might have gone in any direction at that moment, and yet it went in that direction. And why? Probably because as one left the comfort and security of one masculine state, the solitariness, the panic of being on one's own, of truly making one's own way, of really making decisions for oneself, was such that one ran weeping with relief to the next state of masculine power with its illusory stability.

Men seem reluctant to put themselves outside recognised roles in order to improvise new ways of being. We have never used a do-it-yourself approach to our masculinity. To try to create an entirely new model might draw attention to our own lack of mechanical skills and the shoddiness of the original. As it is, we just ask for the latest model, as we did last year, and affect not to notice that the only thing that has changed is the colour of the trim, and that we have had to work twice as hard to afford it anyway. Asked to define the 'DIY feminist', Kathy Bail obliged with a caricature:

> [S]he always has the right line when a bloke at work makes a sexist comment; she has a modem; she knows how to fix the

spin cycle on her washing machine; she keeps a vibrator by the
bed; she plays guitar[;] ... she believes action — from the
bedroom to the boardroom — is everything ... [but most of
all] she is full of contradictions.[30]

Most men would be loath to find themselves caught out in a contradiction on a rainy day.

As yet there is no Generation M to effect a rapprochement with Generation F. We don't want to face feminism; we would far prefer to have it fade away, so that finally we can feel as we felt before. But we are being forced to confront a new phenomenon in our lives, women with new-found confidence, and where, oh where is ours all of a sudden? Can we rediscover any 'certainty and confidence about being male'?[31] Is it possible that, rather than being trapped into the 'sterile choice between celebration and negation'[32] of masculinity, we can find a workable middle ground?

Certainly in reviewing the sites of conflict between the sexes, it is clear that there are two areas in which men and women could effect quite rapid improvement for the better: the home and the workplace. As Hillary Clinton observed in her speech at the Sydney Opera House during her visit to Australia, men and women can share 'concerns about enhancing the qualities of our lives, about raising children, about meeting the demands of work and family'. She also observed that

> so-called 'women's issues' mattered because — at root — they
> were about the way that men and women live together and in
> society ... Because they are about real issues on people's minds
> — kitchen table issues ... [they are therefore] about how
> public and private power should be balanced to address them.

Conclusion

By becoming interested and involved fathers, and supportive responsive colleagues, men can immediately begin to vary and develop in constructive ways.

THE COST OF MASCULINISATION

When I mentioned in the introduction that men needed a wider permission, I was not suggesting that they needed more latitude for the exercise of their power to further cement their present privilege. Men need to return to early areas of hurt in their lives to reclaim aspects of themselves that have been lost, buried or wilfully suppressed by the operation of masculinisation in their lives. A recognition of the pain caused by masculinisation will also allow a glimpse of the additional pain and disadvantages suffered by women, which might act as a basis for an approach to women based on a readiness to listen more acutely to their experience and recast the relationships that we have with them along more equitable lines.

To explore the pun on male/mail in the book's title, we need to open the letter of masculinity that is handed from generation to generation, and carefully examine its contents. Does it have aspects that we can identify as helpful and worthy of being handed on to our sons and supporting in our brothers? Let us retain those. Are there any aspects which appal us, and which we can see as damaging to ourselves and others? Discard them. To carry the envelope of masculinity unopened through our lives shows our fear of what it might contain, and our reluctance to critically examine our gender inheritance. To go to the other extreme, and regard masculinity as 'junk male', discarding it totally, is impractical. However, we can say no to its worst aspects, thus consigning them to the dead letter office of gender history. Now we know we have a choice, and the chance to rewrite the message that we send on in our turn. The opportunity is ours.

This book is an appeal to the self-interest of men. If men simultaneously reject the efforts of women to draw men's attention to the injustice and inequality that are part of women's experience and their demands for change, and yet also fail to realise that masculinity has its physical and psychic cost in their own lives, then those men are doing no-one justice. If men listen to women in an open manner and recognise the cost that masculinity has in men's lives, as well as women's lives, then those same men might be more open to change. They might be prepared to say that there was something to be gained through the insights of feminism, and that both men and women suffer from the operation of sexism in their lives.

Men who endure frustration through the pressures of masculinity exact that toll a hundredfold on those around them and are still in positions of power in a society structured around their economic, social and political power. Men, therefore, need to give themselves permission to step outside the roles that exist in their lives, even though this will draw the discouraging attentions of other men keen to police gender lines, in order to find a new calm, wholeness and strength within. This will not be a strength that will see them continue to deny women's claims for a differently structured society, but rather a strength that will mean men can listen to criticism, hear its truth, accept its recommendations and, from a position of calm confidence, act to change their own lives for the better, and thus the lives of those around them, whether that be at a personal or political level. For while men are massively insecure about themselves they will continue to react to change with

Conclusion

fear and anger, and there will be little hope of profound and enduring modification.

Men's first and personal task, then, is to overcome the habits of thought and language that mean that we are shut to ourselves. If we can achieve some way of getting round the wordlessness about the personal, then we will unlock the door of self. Rather than using all our usual methods for denying responsibility, we can say yes, sexism does have a cost; we can see it in our own lives and the lives of those around us, especially women and children, and from that point we can begin to restructure our lives. The challenge that women present to us is to be actually present and involved in all our relationships: as fathers, lovers, husbands, brothers, friends and colleagues. Our commitments and our activities must be genuine and acted on as real emotional entities to us, rather than things from which we distance ourselves at a moment's notice in order to manipulate circumstances to our advantage. We need to abandon the laboriously constructed masculine selves we present to the world, and re-imagine the self so that, rather than showing a falsely confident mask to the world, we are prepared to be there in the vulnerable moment, listening and involved.

I do not believe in these ideas as a final position. They are merely an interim report, a communique along the way. They are an invitation to respond, to get involved in negotiations. If masculinity is eternally delayed, never arriving, then we men may as well try to grow up by seeking a more mature dialogue with ourselves and others about what it means to be human.

NOTES

EPIGRAPHS

Introduction
Barry Miles, *William Burroughs: El Hombre Invisible*, London: Virgin, 1993, p. 139.
Brian Jackson, *Fatherhood*, Australia: Allen & Unwin, 1984, p. 67.

Chapter 1
Roland Barthes, *A Lover's Discourse*, Harmondsworth: Penguin, 1990, p. 44.
Robert Drewe, *The Savage Crows*, Sydney: Collins, 1976, p. 59.

Chapter 2
Dostoyevsky, *The Brothers Karamazov*, Harmondsworth: Penguin, 1972, vol. 2, p. 875.
Chester Eagle, *Mapping the Paddocks*, Melbourne: McPhee Gribble, 1985, pp. 12–13.

Chapter 3
Stuart Rintoul, *Ashes of Vietnam*, Melbourne: Mandarin, 1987, p. 43.
Captain A. McLeod (killed in action 5 December 1916), in a letter to his wife, in Bill Gammage, *The Broken Years*, Melbourne: Penguin, 1975, p. 168.

Chapter 4
Terry Wallace, former Hawthorn footballer, quoted in Trevor Grant, 'Stretcher cases', *Herald-Sun*, 29 July 1993, p. 41.
Kelvin Templeton, former Footscray and Melbourne footballer, quoted in Trevor Grant, 'Stretcher cases: the grim truth about football', *Herald-Sun*, 29 May 1993, p. 41.

Chapter 5

Garry Wotherspoon, *City of the Plain*, Sydney: Hale & Iremonger, 1991, p. 43.

Chapter 6

Philip Larkin, 'Toads', in *The Less Deceived*, London: Marvell Press, 1973, p. 32.

George Johnston, *My Brother Jack*, Sydney: Angus & Robertson, 1990, p. 49.

Chapter 7

From the painting by James Gleason, 'On the Destruction of the Face as an Authentic Phenomenon' (1939).

From the painting by Dusan Merak, 'Equator' (1948).

Chapter 8

James McQueen, *Hook's Mountain*, Melbourne: Sun Books, 1983.

John Travers, quoted in Julia Sheppard, *Someone Else's Daughter: The Life and Death of Anita Cobby*, Sydney: Ironbark, 1992, p. 189.

Chapter 9

Isaac Rosenberg, 'On War', in Ian Parsons (ed.), *The Collected Works of Isaac Rosenberg*, London: Chatto & Windus, 1984, p. 107.

William Shakespeare, *Richard II*.

Conclusion

Jean-Jacques Rousseau, *Emile*, London: Dent, 1911, pp. 128–9.

Albert Camus, *The Rebel*, London: Hamish Hamilton, 1963, p. 268.

INTRODUCTION

[1] Peter Spearritt and David Walker, *Australian Popular Culture*, Sydney: Allen & Unwin, 1979, p. 158.

[2] *Age, Good Weekend*, 24 March 1990, p. 17.

[3] Desmond Graham, *Keith Douglas 1920–1944*, Oxford: Oxford University Press, 1974, p. 149.

Notes

[4] Heather Formaini, *Men: The Darker Continent*, London: Mandarin, 1991, p. 10.

[5] Formaini, p. 9.

[6] Andrew Tolson, *The Limits of Masculinity*, London: Tavistock, 1977, p. 9.

[7] Andy Metcalf and Martin Humphries, *The Sexuality of Men*, London: Pluto, 1985, p. 6.

[8] A. B. (Banjo) Paterson, 'The Man from Snowy River', in Clement Semmler (ed.), *A.B. (Banjo) Paterson: Bush Ballads, Poems, Stories and Journalism*, St Lucia, University of Queensland Press, 1992, p. 6.

[9] This response was taken from an examination paper.

[10] Thomas Keneally, *Homebush Boy: A Memoir*, Melbourne: Minerva, 1995, p. 85.

[11] Sylvia Lawson, *The Archibald Paradox*, Melbourne: Penguin, 1987, p. 5.

[12] Manning Clark, *The Puzzles of Childhood*, Melbourne: Penguin, 1990, p. 194.

[13] Jonathan Rutherford, *Men's Silences*, London: Routledge, 1992, p. 2.

[14] Rutherford, pp. 56–7.

[15] Metcalf and Humphries, p. 4.

[16] Brian Jackson, *Fatherhood*, Sydney: Allen & Unwin, 1984, p. 6.

[17] Robert Hughes, *The Fatal Shore*, London: Harvill, 1987, p. 429.

[18] Hughes, p. 464.

[19] Peter Middleton, *The Inward Gaze: Masculinity and Subjectivity in Modern Culture*, London: Routledge, 1992, p. 224.

[20] Victor Seidler, *Recreating Sexual Politics: Men, Feminism and Politics*, London: Routledge, 1991, p. x.

[21] Rowena Chapman and Jonathan Rutherford, *Male Order*, London: Lawrence & Wishart, 1988, p. 52.

[22] Chapman and Rutherford, p. 22.

[23] Seidler, p. 92.

[24] Peter O'Connor, *The Mid-Life Crisis*, Sydney: Sun, 1995, p. 53.

[25] Anthony Easthope, *What a Man's Gotta Do*, London: Paladin, 1986, p. 40.
[26] Chapman and Rutherford, p. 47.
[27] Easthope, p. 19.
[28] David Tacey, 'Reconstructing Masculinity', *Meanjin*, 4 (1990), p. 785.
[29] Middleton, p. 270.
[30] Middleton, p. 157.

CHAPTER 1: BODY

[1] Easthope, p. 14.
[2] Easthope, p. 14.
[3] Linda and Peter Murray, *Michelangelo*, London: Thames & Hudson, 1980, p. 42.
[4] David Dalton, *James Dean: The Mutant King*, Drewe: Plexus, 1974, p. 119.
[5] Dalton, p. 119.
[6] Dalton, p. 234.
[7] Anthony Storr, *Churchill's Black Dog*, p. 9.
[8] Storr, p. 9.
[9] Storr, p. 11.
[10] George Johnston, *My Brother Jack*, Sydney: Angus & Robertson, 1990, pp. 53–4.
[11] Sam Fussell, *Muscle: Confessions of an Unlikely Body-Builder*, London: Cardinal, 1991, p. 48.
[12] Fussell, p. 238.
[13] Fussell, p. 249.
[14] Eric Rolls, *Celebration of the Senses*, Melbourne: Nelson, 1984, p. 105.
[15] Humphries et al., *The Sexuality of Men*, London: Pluto, 1985, pp. 32, 31.
[16] Humphries et al., p. 50.

Notes

[17] Humphries et al., p. 30.
[18] Humphries et al., 63.
[19] John Stoltenberg, *Refusing to Be a Man*, London: Fontana, 1992, pp. 56, 58.
[20] Stoltenberg, p. 57.
[21] Easthope, p. 51.
[22] *Age*, 6 May 1991, p. 1.
[23] *Age*, 6 May 1991, p. 1.
[24] Robert Drewe, *The Bodysurfers*, Sydney: James Fraser, 1983, p. 157.
[25] Tony Moore, *Cry of the Damaged Man*, Melbourne: Picador, 1991, pp. 14, 22, 28.
[26] Moore, p. 11.
[27] Blanche d'Alpuget, *Robert J Hawke: A Biography*, Melbourne: Penguin, 1984, p. 30.

CHAPTER 2: FATHERS

[1] Metcalf and Humphries, p. 20.
[2] Metcalf and Humphries, p. 27.
[3] Formaini, p. 51.
[4] Formaini, p. 51.
[5] Chapman and Rutherford, p. 280.
[6] Tolson, p. 25.
[7] Paul Auster, *The Invention of Solitude*, London: Faber, 1988, p. 17.
[8] Formaini, p. 164.
[9] Chapman and Rutherford, p. 287.
[10] Tolson, p. 25.
[11] Tolson, p. 26.
[12] Manning Clark, *Puzzles of Childhood*, Melbourne: Penguin, 1989, p. 159.
[13] Clark, p. 32.
[14] Clark, p. 56.
[15] Clark, p. 126.

[16] Clark, p. 91.
[17] Dalton, p. 223.
[18] Dalton, p. 228.
[19] Dalton, p. 239.
[20] Dalton, p. 250.
[21] Dalton, p. 255.
[22] Clark, p. 130.
[23] Clark, p. 121.
[24] John Mortimer, *Voyage around My Father*, Harmondsworth: Penguin, 1982, p. 84.
[25] John Colmer, *Australian Autobiography: The Personal Quest*, Melbourne: Oxford University Press, 1989, pp. 52–3.
[26] Garry Kinnane, *George Johnston: A Biography*, Melbourne: Penguin, 1986, p. 3.
[27] John and Dorothy Colmer (eds), *The Penguin Book of Australian Autobiography*, Melbourne: Penguin, 1987, p. 92.
[28] Colmer and Colmer, p. 91.
[29] Clark, p. 152.
[30] Colmer and Colmer, p. 244.
[31] Johnston, pp. 4–5.
[32] Clark, p. 178.
[33] Clark, p. 212.
[34] Colmer, p. 75.
[35] Dalton, p. 162.
[36] Tolson, p. 31.
[37] David Malouf, *Johnno*, Queensland: University of Queensland Press, 1975, pp. 4–5.
[38] Malouf, p. 5.
[39] Lahr, *Prick Up Your Ears*, London: Allen Lane, 1978, p. 65.
[40] Lahr, p. 66.
[41] Clark, p. 213.
[42] Franz Kafka, *Wedding Preparations in the Country*, Harmondsworth: Penguin, 1978, p. 60.

Notes

CHAPTER 3: SOLDIERS

1. Burstall, *The Soldier's Story*, Queensland: University of Queensland Press, 1986, p. 6.
2. Burstall, pp. 6–7.
3. Burstall, p. 7.
4. Bill Gammadge, *The Broken Years*, Melbourne: Penguin, 1974, p. 18.
5. Brian Lewis, *Our War*, Melbourne: Penguin, 1980, p. 153.
6. Henry Gullett, *Not As a Duty Only*, Melbourne: Melbourne University Press, 1976, p. 2.
7. John Carroll, *Token Soldiers*, Victoria: Wildgrass, 1983, p. 17.
8. Michael Frazer, *Nasho*, Melbourne: Aries, 1984, p. 18.
9. Stuart Rintoul, *Ashes of Vietnam*, Melbourne: Mandarin, 1987, p. 12.
10. Carroll, p. 4.
11. Carroll, p. 127.
12. Carroll, p. 87.
13. Carroll, p. 87.
14. Rintoul, p. 21.
15. Rintoul, p. 21.
16. Rintoul, p. 3.
17. John Costello, *Love, Sex and War: 1939–1945*, London: Pan, 1985, p. 156.
18. Rintoul, p. 60.
19. Quoted in John Keegan, *The Face of Battle*, Harmondsworth: Penguin, 1976, p. 72.
20. Rintoul, p. 17.
21. Keegan, pp. 71–72.
22. Rintoul, p. 75.
23. Michael Herr, *Dispatches*, London: Picador, 1978, p. 120.
24. Rintoul, p. 216.
25. Gibson in Rintoul, p. 3.
26. Rintoul, p. 85.

27. Windsor, *Memories of the Assassination Attempt*, Melbourne: Penguin, 1985, pp. 175–83.
28. Szapiel in Rintoul, p. 204.
29. Rintoul, p. 194.
30. Rintoul, p. 134.
31. Johnston, p. 17.
32. Peter Pierce, Geoff Doyle and Jeffrey Grey, *Vietnam Days*, Melbourne: Penguin, 1991, p. 63.
33. Peter Cochrane, *Simpson and His Donkey*, Melbourne: Melbourne University Press, 1992, p. 4.
34. Ward, *The Australian Legend, the Making of a Legend*, Melbourne: Oxford University Press, 1964, p. 1.
35. Cochrane, p. 34.
36. Ian McNeill, *The Team: Australian Army Advisors in Vietnam 1962–72*, Canberra: Australian War Memorial, 1984, p. 323.
37. Cochrane, pp. 109–10.

CHAPTER 4: SPORT

1. Peter Boardman, *The Shining Mountain*, London: Hodder & Stoughton, 1978, p. 128.
2. David Craig, *Native Stones*, London: Flamingo, 1987, p. 52.
3. Craig, p. 59.
4. Craig, p. 165.
5. Craig, p. 68.
6. Boardman, p. 123.
7. Roger Bourne, 'Roo Point', *Rock*, 1985, p. 31.
8. For a fuller account, see *Wild*, 3 (1987) and *Rock*, (1987).
9. *Rock*, 1985, pp. 18–21.
10. Jean Bedford and Rose Creswell, *Colouring In*, Melbourne: Penguin, 1986, p. 19.

Notes

[11] I am indebted to Antony Easthope, *What a Man's Gotta Do*, London: Paladin, 1986, for this definition; see pp. 87–8 for his discussion of banter as part of male style.

[12] Craig, p. 47.

[13] Peter Boardman, *Sacred Summits*, London: Arena, 1982, p. 190.

[14] Boardman, *Sacred Summits*, p. 190.

[15] Boardman, *Sacred Summits*, p. 162.

[16] Boardman, *Sacred Summits*, p. 115.

[17] Craig, p. 61.

[18] Geoff Birtles (ed.), *Alan Rouse: A Climber's Life*, London: Unwin, p. 38.

[19] Boardman, *The Shining Mountain*, p. 24.

[20] Boardman, *The Shining Mountain*, p. 61.

[21] Boardman, *The Shining Mountain*, p. 103.

[22] Boardman, *The Shining Mountain*, p. 127.

[23] Boardman, *The Shining Mountain*, p. 54.

[24] Boardman, *The Shining Mountain*, p. 89.

[25] Boardman, *The Shining Mountain*, pp. 77–8.

[26] Boardman, *The Shining Mountain*, p. 148.

[27] Boardman, *The Shining Mountain*, p. 80.

[28] Boardman, *The Shining Mountain*, p. 129.

[29] Boardman, *The Shining Mountain*, p. 107.

[30] Boardman, *The Shining Mountain*, p. 83.

[31] Boardman, *The Shining Mountain*, p. 83.

[32] Boardman, *The Shining Mountain*, p. 83.

[33] Boardman, *The Shining Mountain*, p. 83.

[34] Joe Tasker, *Savage Arena*, London: Methuen, 1982, p. 106.

[35] Boardman, *The Shining Mountain*, p. 105.

[36] Boardman, *The Shining Mountain*, p. 107.

[37] Boardman, *The Shining Mountain*, p. 68.

[38] Jim Curran, *K2: Triumph and Tragedy*, London: Grafton, 1987, p. 173.

CHAPTER 5: OTHER MEN

[1] Martin Amis, *The Moronic Inferno*, Harmondsworth: Penguin, 1986, p. 197.
[2] Amis, p. 191.
[3] Judith Womersley, 'Festival with a message', *Age*, 21 January 1990, p. 11.
[4] Robert Dessaix, 'Gay writing grapples with breaking out of the ghetto', *Sunday Herald*, nd.
[5] Robert Hughes, *The Fatal Shore*, p. 266.
[6] Hughes, p. 536.
[7] Hughes, p. 271.
[8] Wotherspoon, *City of the Plain*, Sydney: Hale & Iremonger, 1991, p. 28.
[9] Hughes, p. 320.
[10] Patsy Adam-Smith, *The Anzacs*, Melbourne: Sphere, 1981, p. 235.
[11] I am indebted to Dennis Altman's reading of this in his article 'The Myth of Mateship', *Meanjin*, 2 (1987), p. 164.
[12] Ken Gelder and Paul Salzman, *The New Diversity*, Melbourne: Penguin, 1989, p. 181.
[13] Dessaix, p. 31.
[14] Randolph Stow, *The Merry-Go-Round in the Sea*, Harmondsworth: Penguin, 1977, p. 274.
[15] Malouf, *Johnno*, p. 154.
[16] Frank Moorhouse, *The Everlasting Secret Family*, Sydney: Imprint, 1988, pp. 167–8.
[17] David Malouf, *Antipodes*, London: Chatto & Windus, 1985, p. 12.
[18] Malouf, *Antipodes*, p. 13.
[19] Malouf, *Antipodes*, p. 24.
[20] Stephen Kirby, 'Homosocial Desire and Homosexual Panic in the Fiction of David Malouf and Frank Moorehouse', *Meanjin*, 3 (1987), p. 391.
[21] Wotherspoon, p. 181.

Notes

22. Michael Kaufman (ed.), *Beyond Patriarchy: Essays by Men on Power, Pleasure and Change*, Toronto: Oxford University Press, 1987, p. 104.
23. John Stoltenberg, *Refusing to be a Man*, London: Fontana, 1989, p. 187.
24. Stoltenberg, p. 186.
25. Stoltenberg, p. 179.
26. Chester Eagle, *Play Together, Dark Blue Twenty*, Melbourne: McPhee Gribble, 1986, pp. 134–5.

CHAPTER 6: WORK

1. Formaini, pp. 127, 129.
2. Formaini, p. 128.
3. Formaini, p. 125.
4. Formaini, p. 129.
5. Brian Adams, *Such Is Life*, Melbourne: Hutchinson, 1987, p. 8.
6. Metcalf and Humphries, p. 111.
7. Tolson, p. 48.
8. Tolson, p. 48.
9. Chapman and Rutherford, p. 280.
10. Tolson, p. 56.
11. Tolson, p. 78.
12. Tolson, p. 75.
13. Gordon Burn, *Somebody's Husband, Somebody's Son*, London: Heinemann, 1984, pp. 123–4.
14. Geoffrey Dutton, *Kenneth Slessor*, Melbourne: Viking, 1991, p. 7.
15. Tolson, p. 53.
16. David Ireland, *The Unknown Industrial Prisoner*, Sydney: Sirius, 1988, p. 235.
17. Ireland, p. 80.
18. Tolson, p. 53.
19. Tolson, p. 59.

[20] Johnston, p. 65.
[21] Johnston, p. 66.
[22] *Sunday Age*, 9 May 1997; see also the *Age*, 8 October 1991, p. 3; a 'toilet prank' at a Braybrook factory, in which two workmates lit paint thinner they had poured on a toilet cubicle's floor, resulted in an apprentice suffering serious burns to his face, hands and buttocks. Jokes at the factory were 'very much the order of the day', and the employee who did it had seen it done seven or eight times before, having twice been a victim of the same prank himself.
[23] Metcalf and Humphries, p. 123.
[24] Norman Aisbett, 'Bus depot hostility tests sex discrimination laws', *West Australian*, 8 March 1993, pp. 4–5.
[25] Metcalf and Humphries, p. l25.
[26] Metcalf and Humphries, p. 125.
[27] Jeff Hearn, *The Sexuality of Organization*, London: Sage, p. 95.
[28] Hearn, p. 97.
[29] Tolson, p. 61.
[30] Hearn, p. 98.
[31] Ireland, p. 267.
[32] Tolson, p. 82.
[33] Tolson, p. 82.
[34] Tolson, p. 103.
[35] Tolson, p. 104.
[36] Formaini, p. 115.
[37] Seidler, p. 125.
[38] *Age*, 27 June 1992, p. 18.
[39] Ireland, p. 80.

CHAPTER 7: ARTIST

[1] Dutton, pp. 17–18.
[2] Storr, *Churchill's Black Dog*, Glasgow: Collins, 1988, p. 77.

Notes

[3] Ann Charters, *Kerouac*, London: Picador, 1973, p. 91.
[4] John Lahr, *Dame Edna and the Rise of Western Civilisation*, London: Bloomsbury, 1991, p. 36.
[5] Andrew Motion, *The Lamberts: George, Constant and Kit*, London: Hogarth, 1987, p. 18.
[6] Motion, p. 65.
[7] Steven Naifeh and Gregory White Smith, *Jackson Pollock*, London: Pimlico, 1990, p. 20.
[8] Humphrey McQueen, *Suburbs of the Sacred*, Melbourne: Penguin, 1988, p. 157.
[9] Motion, p. 24.
[10] Brian Kiernan, *David Williamson: A Writer's Career*, Melbourne: William Heinemann, 1990, p. 26.
[11] Kiernan, p. 182.
[12] Lahr, p. 60.
[13] Johnston, p. 92.
[14] Motion, p. 98.
[15] Motion, p. 89.
[16] Motion, p. 82.
[17] Richard Haese, *Rebels and Precursors: The Revolutionary Years of Australian Art*, Melbourne: Penguin, 1988, p. 15.
[18] Alister Kershaw, *Hey Days: Memories and Glimpses of Melbourne's Bohemia 1937–1947*, Sydney: Imprint, 1991, p. 3.
[19] Dutton, p. 310.
[20] Haese, p. 13.
[21] Adams, p. 34.
[22] Haese, p. 52.
[23] John Larkin, 'Money and enemies', *Sunday Age*, 1 March 1992, p. 6.
[24] Larkin, p. 6.
[25] Kiernan, p. 319.
[26] Kiernan, p. 265.
[27] Haese, p. 19.

[28] Stewart Cameron, 'Art's just not the norm for blokes', *Australian*, 21 February 1992, p. 3.
[29] Haese, p. 119.
[30] Haese, p. 119.
[31] Adams, p. 42.
[32] See Adams, pp. 38–40, for this account.
[33] Larkin.
[34] Sonya Voumard, 'David Williamson no longer the "rat" who "left"', *Age*, 21 March 1992, p. 5.
[35] Naifeh and Smith, p. 170.

CHAPTER 8: MURDER

[1] Deborah Cameron and Elizabeth Frazer, *The Lust to Kill*, Cambridge: Polity, 1987, p. xii.
[2] Rosalind Miles, *Rites of Man*, London: Paladin, 1992, p. 267.
[3] Miles, p. 271.
[4] Andrew Rule, *Cuckoo*, Melbourne: Floradale, 1988, p. 199.
[5] Leslie Kennedy and Mark Whittaker, *Granny Killer: The Story of John Glover*, Melbourne: Collins/Angus & Robertson, 1992, p. 94.
[6] Kennedy and Whittaker, p. 104.
[7] Cameron and Frazer, p. 16.
[8] Julia Sheppard, *Someone Else's Daughter: The Life and Death of Anita Cobby*, Sydney: Ironbark, 1992, p. 18.
[9] Coronial papers in the Queen Street case; all subsequent unacknowledged quotations in the Vitkovic case are drawn from this source.
[10] Colin Wilson and Donald Seaman, *The Serial Killers*, London: W. H. Allen, 1990, p. 186.
[11] Matthew Ricketson, 'Silent madness', *Australian Magazine*, 3–4 December 1988, p. 24.
[12] Anthony Storr, *Solitude*, London: Flamingo, 1989, p. 37.

Notes

[13] The details of Knight's life put forward here are mainly drawn from the Proceedings of the Supreme Court in *The Crown v. Knight*, 28 October 1988.

[14] Sheppard, p. 18.

[15] Sheppard, p. 19.

[16] Tess Lawrence, 'Confessions of the Hoddle Street killer', *Age Good Weekend*, 3 December 1988, p. 50.

[17] Lawrence Miller and Bill Ayres, 'The self pitying monster of Hoddle Street', *New Idea*, 22 February 1992, p. 35.

[18] Wilson and Seaman, p. 281.

[19] Heather Strang, *Homicide in Australia 1990–1991*, Sydney: Australian Institute of Criminology, 1992, p. 13.

[20] Kenneth Polk and David Ransom, 'Homicide in Victoria' in Chappel and Grabovsky (eds), *Australian Violence: Contemporary Perspectives*, Australian Institute of Criminology, 1991, p. 54.

[21] Strang, p. 13.

[22] Polk and Ransom, p. 69.

[23] Miles, p. 271.

[24] Polk and Ransom, p. 79.

[25] Ann Jones, *Women Who Kill*, London: Gollancz, 1991, p. 368.

[26] Polk and Ransom, p. 79.

[27] Polk and Ransom, p. 71.

[28] Russell Coulson, 'Killer's threat to behead wife', *Herald-Sun*, 29 May 1992, p. 25.

[29] David Ireland, *City of Women*, Melbourne: Penguin, 1983, pp. 153–4.

[30] Miles, p. 18.

[31] Polk and Ransom; I am indebted to this article for the information on Luckenbill and confrontational homicide.

[32] Polk and Ransom, p. 101.

[33] Polk and Ransom, p. 95.

[34] Christine Adler, 'Explaining Violence: Socioeconomics and Masculinity' in Chappell and Grabovsky (eds), *Australian Violence: Contemporary Perspectives*, p. 167.

[35] Anita Quigley, 'Student kill bid', *Herald-Sun*, 14 August 1992.
[36] Brian Masters, *Killing for Company*, p. 262.
[37] Kennedy and Whittaker, p. 206.
[38] Wilson and Seaman, p. 295.
[39] Wilson and Seaman, p. 295.

CHAPTER 9: SUICIDE

[1] Miles, p. 258.
[2] Miles, p. 94.
[3] Fiona Athersmith, '"Surfer" contributed to death: Coroner', *Age*, 22 August l991, p. 5.
[4] Robert Kosky, 'Is Suicidal Behaviour Increasing among Australian Youth?, *Medical Journal of Australia*, 147, (1987), p. 165.
[5] Chris Wallace, 'Field of dreams', *Who*, 22 April 1992, pp. 26–7.
[6] Anthony Davis and Cas Schrueder, 'The Prediction of Suicide' *Medical Journal of Australia*, 153, (1990), p. 552.
[7] Davis and Schrueder, p. 554.
[8] Michael Dudley et al., 'Youth Suicide in New South Wales: Urban–Rural Trends', *Medical Journal of Australia*, 156, (1992), p. 83.
[9] Dudley et al., p. 86.
[10] A. Martina, 'Suicide and Unemployment among Young Australian Males 1966–1986', Working Paper No. 56, Department of Economic History, Australian National University, Canberra, 1985, p.50.
[11] Riaz Hassan and Joan Carr, 'Changing Patterns of Suicide in Australia', *Australian and New Zealand Journal of Psychiatry*, 23, (1989), p. 227.
[12] Hassan and Carr, p. 227.
[13] Dudley et al., p. 86.
[14] Dudley et al., p. 86.
[15] Dudley et al., p. 87.
[16] Hassan and Carr, p. 228.

Notes

[17] John Lindsay, 'Australian Suicidology', *Australian and New Zealand Journal of Psychiatry*, 12 (1978), p. 176.

[18] A. Alvarez, *The Savage God: A Study of Suicide*, Harmondsworth: Penguin, 1975, p. 269.

[19] Alvarez, p. 43.

[20] Miles, p. 259.

[21] Miles, p. 258.

[22] Danny Power, Terry Brown and Adrian Dunn, 'Trots champ tragedy', *Herald-Sun*, 10 April 1991, pp. 1, 2; see also Richard Trembath, 'Pacing: Post Vin Knight', *Sunday Age*, 'Focus', 18 August 1991, p. 21.

[23] Mark Chipperfield and Mike Safe, 'The Podgornik riddle', *Australian Magazine*, 28–29 April 1990, pp. 8–18; see also Elizabeth Minter, 'Podgornik committed suicide, says court', *Age*, 11 November 1990.

[24] John O'Neill, 'When a uniform can't hide the pain', *Sunday Age*, 21 January 1990, p. 5.

[25] Miles, p. 258.

[26] Hassan and Carr, pp. 230, 231.

[27] Hassan and Carr, p. 231.

[28] Kosky, p. 165.

[29] *Bulletin*, 10 December 1989, p. 47.

[30] Australian Bureau of Statistics, *Causes of Death, 1987*, AGPS, 1988.

[31] Anthony Davis, 'Suicidal Behaviour among Adolescents: Its Nature and Prevention' in R. Kosky et al., *Breaking Out: Challenges in Adolescent Mental Health in Australia*, AGPS, 1992, p. 95.

[32] Hassan and Carr, pp. 226–7.

[33] Miles, p. 22.

[34] Hassan and Carr, p. 268.

[35] Dudley et al., p. 84.

[36] Robert J. Goldney, 'Suicide in Young Persons', *Medical Journal of Australia*, 147 (1987), p. 161.

[37] Dudley et al., p. 87.

[38] Anthony Davis, 'Attempted Suicide in Adelaide and Perth', *Medical Journal of Australia*, 154 (1991), p. 668.
[39] Miles, p. 4.
[40] Alvarez, p. 270.
[41] Miles, p. 4.

CONCLUSION

[1] Rutherford, p. 129.
[2] Rutherford, p. 127.
[3] Bev Roberts, 'Variations on the Convention' in *Australian Book Review*, April 1992, p. 10.
[4] Rutherford, p. 9.
[5] T. R. Edmonds, *North and West of Melrose Street*, Sydney: Simon & Schuster, 1993, p. 3.
[6] Edmonds, p. 12.
[7] Edmonds, p. 75.
[8] Edmonds, p. 74.
[9] Edmonds, p. 210.
[10] Jill Ker Conway, *Written by Herself*, New York: Vintage, 1992, p. viii.
[11] Colmer, p. 10.
[12] Clive James, *Unreliable Memoirs*, London: Picador, 1980, p. 142.
[13] James, p. 64.
[14] James, p. 100.
[15] James, p. 33.
[16] James, p. 16.
[17] Fay Zwicky, *The Lyre in the Pawnshop*, Perth: University of Western Australia Press, 1986, p. 179.
[18] Cyril Connolly, *Enemies of Promise*, Harmondsworth: Penguin, 1979, p. 157.
[19] Seidler, p. 96.
[20] Zwicky, p. 162.

Notes

[21] Zwicky, p. 170.
[22] Zwicky, p. 175.
[23] Alan Moorehead, *A Late Education*, Harmondsworth: Penguin, 1970, p. 22.
[24] Stephen Knight, 'Real Pulp at Last', *Meanjin*, 4 (1986), p. 446.
[25] Peter Corris, *Matrimonial Causes*, Sydney: Bantam, 1993, pp. 12–13.
[26] Tacey, p. 790.
[27] Michael Gow, *Away*, Sydney: Currency, 1995, p. 39.
[28] Ronald Hayman, *Nietzsche: A Critical Biography*, London: Phoenix, 1995, p. 172.
[29] Robert Dessaix, *A Mother's Disgrace*, Sydney: Angus & Robertson, 1994, p. 27.
[30] Michelle Gunn, 'A good time in history for young feminists doing it for themselves', *Australian*, 23 October 1996, p. 4.
[31] Peter West, *Fathers, Lovers and Sons*, Sydney: Finch, 1996, p. 5.
[32] R. W. Connell, *Masculinities*, St Leonard's: Allen & Unwin, 1995, p. 239.

BIBLIOGRAPHY

This bibliography is organised into three sections: the theoretical works on which the book is based, the life narratives used to illustrate the book, and books that were of value in supplying the cultural context. The life narratives used include autobiography, semi-autobiographical fiction, fiction, and biography by and about men.

The bibliography contains only book-length works.

THEORETICAL PERSPECTIVES

This section is an overview of writings on masculinity from a variety of viewpoints, from Australia, America and England.

Al Alvarez, *The Savage God: A Study of Suicide*, Harmondsworth: Penguin, 1975.

Steve Biddulph, *Manhood: A Book About Setting Men Free*, Sydney: Finch, 1994.

Robert Bly, *Iron John*, New York: Addison Wesley, 1990.

David Buchbinder, *Masculinities and Identities*, Melbourne: Melbourne University Press, 1994.

Rowena Chapman and Jonathan Rutherford, *Male Order*, London: Lawrence & Wishart, 1988.

David Cohen, *Being a Man*, London: Routledge, 1990.

Terry Colling, *Beyond Mateship: Understanding Australian Men*, Sydney: Simon & Schuster, 1992.

R. W. Connell, *Masculinities*, Sydney: Allen & Unwin, 1995.

Ronald Conway, *Being Male: A Guide for Masculinity, in a Time of Change*, Melbourne: Macmillan, 1985.

Antony Easthope, *What a Man's Gotta Do*, London: Paladin, 1986.

Heather Formaini, *Men: The Darker Continent*, London: Mandarin, 1991.

Michael Gilding, *The Making and Breaking of the Australian Family*, Sydney: Allen & Unwin, 1991.

Jeff Hearn, Deborah Sheppard, Tancred-Sheriff and Gibson Burrell, *The Sexuality of Organisation*, London: Sage, 1989.

Brian Jackson, *Fatherhood*, Sydney: Allen & Unwin, 1984.

Ann Jones, *Women Who Kill*, London: Gollancz, 1991.

Michael Kaufman (ed.), *Beyond Patriarchy: Essays by Men on Pleasure, Power and Change*, Toronto: Oxford, 1987.

Sam Keen, *Fire in the Belly: On Being a Man*, New York: Bantam, 1991.

Jodey Kewley, *Fathers: Sixteen Men Tell How They Really Feel about Fatherhood*, Melbourne: McPhee Gribble, 1993.

Andy Metcalf and Martin Humphries, *The Sexuality of Men*, London: Pluto, 1985.

Peter Middleton, *The Inward Gaze: Masculinity and Subjectivity in Modern Culture*, London: Routledge, 1992.

Rosalind Miles, *Rites of Man*, London: Paladin, 1992.

John Money, *Gay, Straight and In Between*, New York: Oxford University Press, 1988.

David Porter, *Between Men and Feminism*, London: Routledge, 1992.

Jonathan Rutherford, *Men's Silences: Predicaments in Masculinity*, London: Routledge, 1992.

Jocelynne Scutt, *Growing Up Feminist: The New Generation of Australian Women*, Sydney: Angus & Robertson, 1985.

Lynne Segal, *Slow Motion: Changing Masculinities, Changing Men*, London: Virago, 1990.

Victor Seidler (ed.), *The Achilles Heel Reader: Men, Sexual Politics and Socialism*, London: Routledge, 1991.

Victor Seidler, *Recreating Sexual Politics: Men, Feminism and Politics*, London: Routledge, 1991.

John Stoltenberg, *Refusing to Be a Man*, London: Fontana, 1989.

Bibliography

Heather Strang, *Homicides in Australia 1990–1991*, Canberra: Australian Institute of Criminology, 1992.
Andrew Tolson, *The Limits of Masculinity*, London: Tavistock, 1977.
Peter West, *Fathers, Lovers and Sons*, Sydney: Finch, 1996.
Garry Wotherspoon, *City of the Plain: History of a Gay Sub-Culture*, Sydney: Hale & Iremonger, 1991.
Fay Zwicky, *The Lyre in the Pawnshop*, Perth: University of Western Australia Press, 1986.

LIFE NARRATIVES

The life narratives of men trace the struggles of men to achieve an appropriate masculine persona, and Australia produces many records of such struggles. Three theoretical works of interest precede the list of narratives used in the text.

John Colmer, *Australian Autobiography: The Personal Quest*, Melbourne: Oxford University Press, 1989.
John Colmer and Dorothy Colmer (eds), *The Penguin Book of Australian Autobiography*, Melbourne: Penguin, 1987.
David McCooey, *Artful Histories: Modern Australian Autobiographies*, Melbourne: CUP, 1996.

Brian Adams, *Such Is Life: A Biography of Sidney Nolan*, Melbourne: Hutchinson, 1987.
Brian Adams, *William: Portrait of an Artist*, Sydney: Vintage, 1983.
John Carroll, *Token Soldiers*, Melbourne: Wildgrass, 1983.
Manning Clark, *The Puzzles of Childhood*, Melbourne: Penguin, 1989.
Blanche d'Alpuget, *Robert J. Hawke: A Biography*, Melbourne: Penguin, 1984.
Robert Dessaix, *A Mother's Disgrace*, Sydney: Angus & Robertson, 1994.
Geoffrey Dutton, *Kenneth Slessor*, Melbourne: Viking, 1991.
Chester Eagle, *Play Together, Dark Blue Twenty*, Melbourne: McPhee Gribble, 1986.

Junk Male

T. R. Edmonds, *North and West of Melrose Street*, Sydney: Simon & Schuster, 1993.

A. B. Facey, *A Fortunate Life*, Melbourne: Penguin, 1989.

Michael Frazer, *Nasho*, Melbourne: Aries, 1984.

David Ireland, *The Unknown Industrial Prisoner*, Sydney: Sirius, 1988.

Clive James, *Unreliable Memoirs*, London: Picador, 1980.

George Johnston, *My Brother Jack*, Sydney: Angus & Robertson, 1990.

Alister Kershaw, *Hey Days: Memories and Glimpses of Melbourne's Bohemia 1937–1947*, Sydney: Imprint, 1991.

John Kingsmill, *The Innocent*, Sydney: Imprint, 1990.

Garry Kinnane, *George Johnston: A Biography*, Melbourne: Penguin, 1986.

John Lahr, *Dame Edna and the Rise of Western Civilisation*, London: Bloomsbury, 1991.

John Lahr, *Prick Up Your Ears*, Harmondsworth: Penguin, 1980.

Brian Lewis, *Our War*, Melbourne: Penguin, 1980.

Mary Lord, *Hal Porter: Man of Many Parts*, Sydney: Random House, 1993.

Sandra McGrath, *Brett Whiteley*, Sydney: Angus & Robertson, 1992.

Peter McMillan, *Men, Sex and Other Secrets*, Melbourne: Text, 1992.

David Malouf, *Antipodes*, London: Chatto & Windus, 1985.

David Malouf, *Johnno*, Melbourne: Penguin, 1987.

Tony Moore, *Cry of the Damaged Man*, Melbourne: Picador, 1991.

Alan Moorehead, *A Late Education*, Harmondsworth: Penguin, 1970.

Frank Moorhouse, *The Everlasting Secret Family*, Sydney: Imprint, 1988.

Andrew Motion, *The Lamberts: George, Constant and Kit*, London: Hogarth, 1987.

Lloyd Rees, *Peaks and Valleys*, Sydney: Angus & Robertson, 1993.

Andrew Riemer, *Inside, Outside*, Sydney: Imprint, 1992.

Stuart Rintoul, *Ashes of Vietnam*, Melbourne: Mandarin, 1987.

Eric Rolls, *Celebration of the Senses*, Melbourne: Nelson, 1984.

Sasha Soldatow, *Private — Do Not Open*, Melbourne: Penguin, 1987.

Bibliography

BACKGROUND READING

The following works provided helpful background reading.

Patsy Adam-Smith, *The Anzacs*, Melbourne: Sphere, 1981.

Judith Brett, *Robert Menzies' Forgotten People*, Sydney: Pan Macmillan, 1992.

Deborah Cameron and Elizabeth Frazer, *The Lust to Kill*, Cambridge: Polity, 1987.

Martin Flanagan, *Southern Sky, Western Oval: A Year Inside League Football*, Melbourne: McPhee Gribble, 1994.

Bill Gammage, *The Broken Years*, Melbourne: Penguin, 1974.

Ken Gelder and Paul Salzman, *The New Diversity: Australian Fiction 1970–1988*, Melbourne: Penguin, 1989.

Robin Gerster, *Big-Noting: The Heroic Theme in Australian War Writing*, Melbourne: Melbourne University Press, 1987.

Noel Giblett (ed.), *Homecomings: Stories from Vietnam Veterans and Their Wives*, Canberra: AGPS, 1990.

Jeffrey Grey and Jeff Doyle, *Vietnam: War, Myth and Memory*, Sydney: Allen & Unwin, 1992.

Richard Haese, *Rebels and Precursors: The Revolutionary Years of Australian Art*, Melbourne: Penguin, 1988.

Christopher Heathcote, *A Quiet Revolution: The Rise of Australian Art 1946–1968*, Melbourne: Text, 1995.

Robert Hughes, *The Fatal Shore*, London: Harvill, 1987.

Robert Kosky, Hadi Eshkevari and Garry Kneebone, *Breaking Out: Challenges in Adolescent Mental Health in Australia*, Canberra: AGPS, 1992.

Janet McCalman, *Struggletown: Portrait of an Australian Working Class Community 1900–1965*, Melbourne: Penguin, 1988.

Humphrey McQueen, *Suburbs of the Sacred: Transforming Australian Belief and Values*, Melbourne: Penguin, 1988.

Greg Pemberton, *Vietnam Remembered*, Sydney: Weldon, 1990.

Jane Ross, *The Myth of the Digger: The Australian Soldiers in Two World Wars*, Sydney: Hale & Iremonger, 1985.

Andrew Rule, *Cuckoo*, Melbourne: Floradale, 1988.

Kay Schaffer, *Women and the Bush*, Melbourne: Cambridge University Press, 1988.

Julia Sheppard, *Someone Else's Daughter: The Life and Death of Anita Cobby*, Sydney: Ironbark, 1992.

Nancy D. H. Underhill, *Making Australian Art: Sydney Ure Smith, Patron and Publisher*, Melbourne: Oxford University Press, 1991.

Bill Williams and Gisela Gardener, *Men: Sex, Power and Survival*, Melbourne: Greenhouse, 1989.

ACKNOWLEDGEMENTS

Our thanks go to those who have given us permission to reproduce copyright material in this book. Particular sources of print material are acknowledged in the text.

Every effort has been made to contact the copyright holders of text material. The publisher welcomes communication from any copyright holder from whom permission was inadvertently not gained.

Extracts from *North and West of Melrose Street* by T.R. Edmunds, published by Simon and Schuster Australia, permission courtesy of the author.

Excerpts from *The Face of Battle* by John Keegan. Copyright © 1976 by John Keegan. Used by permission of Viking Penguin, a division of Penguin Books USA Inc.